For the Record

Past~Forward Memoir Writers of Charleston, Illinois

ISBN: 978-1-945567-33-9
Library of Congress: 2021918804
Cover Art by Jessica Mertz
Cover Design by Pam Daniel

DEDICATION

We dedicate our third book, *For the Record*, to four beloved Past~Forward members who have passed away since the publication of *The Memory Pool: Reflections of Past~Forward*: Bob Clapp, Madeline Ignazito, Johnni Olds, and Julia Rea. Your memories live on in your beautiful, heart-felt, and inspiring writing.

CONTENTS

Page:

ACKNOWLEDGMENTS

First and foremost, we thank the writers who contributed to this book with their entertaining, thought-provoking, and insightful personal essays and poems. Thank you to the Coles County Arts Council, our sponsors, for their continued support of Past~Forward throughout the years. We are fortunate to have such a vital arts organization in our community.

This book would not have been possible without June Hayden and Janet Messenger, who spear-headed this labor of love. As co-chairs of the Publishing Committee, they worked with committee members Phyllis Bayles, Shelley Crouch, Bill Heyduck, and Amy Lynch to find the best publisher, editors, and graphic designers for the book. All worked tirelessly to promote *For the Record*.

The Editing Committee, made up of Charlotte England, Daiva Markelis, and Marita Metzke, read all submitted creative work, did preliminary editing, communicated with writers, and provided the organizational structure for this volume. Phyllis Bayles directed the book signing program. We thank these individuals for their hard work and enthusiasm.

There was a contest to find the best title for this volume. Past~Forward member Rayma Laughlin came up with the winning *For the Record*.

We are thankful that our publisher, Crystal Heart Imprints, agreed to take on this project. We thank them for their guidance. Big thanks go out to Julian Delfino, who did a great job polishing up the work of our writers, and to Charleston artist Jessica Mertz, who designed our wonderful cover.

We would like to thank the Charleston Carnegie Public Library and Wesley United Methodist Church for providing meeting space for our writers.

We are fortunate to have such supportive family members and friends. We are thankful for all of our fantastic readers who've picked up this book and do so much to support the arts in our community.

Preface

~

June Hayden

The Past~Forward Memoir Writers of Charleston, Illinois are pleased to present their latest volume of memories, poems, anecdotes, and musings. *For the Record* is a compilation of writings from twenty-nine authors with backgrounds as diverse as the stories they share.

My personal introduction to Past~Forward occurred in 2011, when I read a story that appeared in a local newspaper and announced the publication of the group's first book, *Occasional Writers: Bringing the Past Forward*, which contained forty pieces written by sixteen area authors.

The article gave a brief description of some of the stories in the book, and I was particularly interested in those written from a dog's point of view. I wondered what tales my cats might have to tell, should they ever decide to start sharing their stories. As I continued reading the article, I became increasingly excited.

How I longed to meet the authors and attend their monthly meetings. Yet I knew this would not be possible—not, at least, until I retired. Still, I never lost my desire to join the group. And now, ten years later, I am a proud member of the Past~Forward Memoir Writers group and am pleased to introduce our third book. While I never got to meet Milo, I am happy to have become friends with his amanuensis, Janet Messenger, who is a co-founder of the group.

The Past~Forward Memoir Writers trace their beginning to 2008, when six adult students attended the *Introduction to Writing Memoir* class offered by the EIU Academy of Lifelong Learning, taught by Dr. Daiva Markelis. At the end of the five-week session, the students left with a determination to continue recording their personal and family stories. However, they soon found that without the encouragement and support of fellow authors, they weren't getting much writing done. Realizing the importance of networking with other writers, the core members decided to form a memoir-writing group. Led by Janet Messenger, they started meeting at the Charleston Carnegie Public Library the last Friday afternoon of each month and invited interested writers in the community to join them. Now in need of a moniker, the emergent group held a contest to choose a name for itself.

Bill Heyduck, one of the original members and a contributing author to this book, submitted the winning entry, and the group became known as the Past~Forward Memoir Writers. Shortly thereafter, the recently christened group became a part of the Coles County Arts Council, representing the organization's literary division.

As group membership continued to increase, an evening session was added. Capably led by Daiva Markelis, the evening session also provides an opportunity for participation by writers whose schedules do not permit them to attend the afternoon meetings.

The afternoon session remained under the skillful leadership of Janet Messenger until she retired in fall 2020; I now have the honor of leading the afternoon group. Both groups welcome new members. For more information, please feel free to contact Daiva Markelis at dmmarkelis@eiu.edu or June Hayden at jhayden529@gmail.com.

Since the group's inception, its leaders have sought to help members hone their writing skills by inviting guest speakers and hosting writing workshops. Members have shared their stories in public readings at the local library, during visits to area long-term care facilities, and most recently, through Past~Forward's newly created YouTube channel. In addition to its first book, the group also published a second book, *The Memory Pool*, in 2014.

The outbreak of a global pandemic in early 2020 brought myriad challenges to individuals, groups, and businesses around the world. Past~Forward was not exempt from these difficulties. When COVID-related constraints prohibited in-person meetings, the group opted to hold virtual meetings until the restrictions were lifted.

Most members quickly adapted to the new meeting format, and by mid-year, a word that had been previously associated with fast cars and little children at play took on a whole new meaning.

Now, having conquered the realms of cyberspace, Past~Forward members comfortably Zoom across the World Wide Web at speeds measured not in miles per hour but in megabits per second.

In addition to introducing us to the world of Zoom, COVID was also a contributing factor in Past~Forward's latest endeavor — the creation of a YouTube channel. When it became apparent that Past~Forward would not be able to hold its much-anticipated annual public reading, Phyllis Bayles suggested YouTube as an alternative method of sharing stories. She and June Hayden worked together and created a Past~Forward channel, releasing the first YouTube video on December 23, 2020. Since then, the YouTube team has grown to include Amy Lynch and Shelley Crouch. All team members are also contributing authors to this book.

Derived from the French word *mémoire*, meaning memory or reminiscence, the memoir is simply a collection of memories someone writes about his or her own life. A favorite quote of mine comes from George R.R. Martin's *A Dance with Dragons*: "A reader lives a thousand lives before he dies ... The man who never reads lives only one."

I think the quote can also be applied to memoirists. Could it not be said that the memoir writer lives many lives before he dies, while the one who never writes his memories lives only one? In writing our life stories, we relive our lives many times over before passing our memories on to future generations. Our writings travel through time, becoming a bridge to the past and a portal to the future.

The stories in this book cover a variety of topics, from spring tonics to toilet paper. They are insightful, romantic, poignant, and bittersweet. Our members write about winter days and summer nights, about facing fears and finding love. They speak of grief and loss, of courage and triumph—of a mother who summons the strength to carry on in spite of paralyzing grief, and a teenage boy who musters the courage to take a stand against racial prejudice, even though it means disobeying his boss's orders.

Our writers share stories of chasing possums from the chicken house, zip lining through the Oregon rain forest, and coping with the challenges of the pandemic. One mother confesses to almost trampling her child and two innocent bystanders as she scrambles to grab a coveted candy bar during a local parade. And Milo is back, offering canine wisdom to a lovestruck teenager as he tries his "paw" at writing an advice column.

Close your eyes and drift back in time. Hear the music of the Big Band era as you imagine you are dancing beneath a starlit summer sky; inhale the tantalizing aromas of cinnamon, nuts, and honey wafting from a Greek kitchen; and feel the snowflakes tickle your nose as you slide down a hill on a homemade sled fashioned from an old-discarded rocker. These aren't just stories you will read, but memories you will experience right along with the authors.

So pull up a chair, grab a favorite drink, and start living one of your thousand lives. For the record, we are certain the experience is one you are going to enjoy.

Zip-a-Dee-Doo-Dah

~

Jane Gilbert

I am afraid of high places. So why in the world would I want to go zip lining? Because from the first time I saw it on TV, I thought, "That looks like the most exciting thing to do in the whole world." It was a safe thought, since I knew I would never have the opportunity. I could fantasize about it and see myself zipping through the trees without considering reality: pie in the sky!

But recently, while on a river cruise on the West Coast, I was suddenly presented with the chance. For real! Not fantasy, not pie in the sky, but me up there on a rope, looking down. Fantasy meets fear. Can I do it? What's the worst that could happen? It's probably safer than driving a car. Then again, I might panic or have a heart attack or wet my pants and die of shame, but I'm eighty-one years old, and this opportunity will never come around again. Let's go for it!

There were five of us brave souls in the party that day. The youngest was a thirteen-year-old girl, Abbie, brought by a grandfather young enough to be my son. The others were Joann and Trish, two women of middle years eager to try a new adventure. Our guides were two young men, SJ and Bo, both rugged and handsome. They quickly proved to be competent and considerate instructors.

The first step was to get weighed and into a harness. Helmets came next, and all straps were checked and double-checked. The directions were brief: "There will be eight lines—the first one not very long and not very high. You may hold on to your tether, but you don't have to. Just pull up your feet and sit in the harness. Don't try to help us.

"We will do all the work: we will hook you on, stop you, and unhook you. Enjoy the ride!"

A few minutes later, I was standing on a low stump and SJ was hooking me onto the line just a couple of feet above my head. Looking down it, I could see Bo at the other end waiting for me. All I had to do was step off the stump and pull up my feet. It was one of the bravest things I've ever done. I stepped off, and the next thing I knew, I was riding comfortably through the incredibly beautiful Oregon rain forest. Fifteen seconds later, I was back on the ground, laughing with excitement, thrilled and proud and eager to go again.

The lines got progressively longer and higher. By the third one, we were zipping over water. I had stopped thinking about height or fear or anything else except the excitement and joy of the ride. Now SJ told us, "This time, try letting go of the tether. Your harness will hold you. Just don't put your legs up in the air. If you do, you'll go upside down for sure."

I waved and kicked and even dipped my hand in the water on a low pass over a lake—kept my feet down, too, and landed right side up.

Next, we came to the tower. We went up to the top of a hill and then climbed many wooden steps to the first platform. I carefully ignored the stairs leading to a still-higher level. Suddenly, I was thinking about heights again, but not for long. I went first. It was breathtaking. The longest ride yet, and the most spectacular view of this wide landscape. It was not the tropical jungle I had seen watching zip-liners on TV but hilly terrain, heavily forested and lush in its new spring green. I didn't want it to end, but it did all too soon.

I heard the *thunk* of the brake, and I was back on solid ground, watching my adventure-mates sail in with the same excitement I had experienced. We were no longer strangers: we were buddies and already feeling smugly superior to our friends who had chosen not to come along.

Too soon, it was time for the last ride. We found ourselves back at the tower, and this time, we climbed all the way to the top. It was a wide platform, and there were not one but two lines stretching a quarter of a mile over a lake to our final destination back at the starting point. Now SJ explained that we had options. We could go off in the usual way, or, instead of using a two-foot tether, we could use a twenty-foot tether hooked to one of the lines and step off from the starting point of the other. That way, we would swing on our twenty-foot tether back and forth all the way across the lake.

Four of us stood speechless, trying to visualize this — first the long drop and then the swing. But Abbie was jumping up and down, asking, "Grandpa, can I? Can I?" She was the first to go, and we watched in admiration as she swung and shrieked and waved her arms until she was little more than a speck in the distance. At that point, Joann and Trish decided to out-dare each other, and they both followed her example. Did I consider doing it? Maybe for five seconds, but I decided I had pushed myself to the limit already and that prudence was the better part of valor.

Apparently, Grandpa came to the same conclusion. We rode down side by side.

In the van riding back to the boat, I was exhilarated and happy but also a little let down. The adventure was over. Little did I know just how long the repercussions were going to continue. At dinner that night and for the rest of the week, I discovered that strangers wanted to hear about going zip lining.

"Weren't you scared?" they'd say, or "I could never do that, but then they wanted to hear more. I hadn't done it to impress people with my daring, but that seemed to be the result. Back home, I got more of the same from family and friends: "Were you temporarily deranged?" and "You're how old?" I loved it. I would highly recommend zip lining to any senior who wants to feel young and adventuresome and really cool. Or at least appear that way.

Dancing on the Blacktop

~

Bill Heyduck

In the late spring of 1949, a few months before I was to be discharged from the Marine Corps, I came home on a twenty-day leave. I spent the first few days getting reacquainted with my parents and siblings. I hadn't been home in almost two years, and we had all changed to a certain degree. I also needed to start the application process for entering Millikin University, and after that, I could start looking up some of my old buddies who were still in town.

My friends all had jobs and were busy during the day, so we only got together after sundown. The first night, we all sat around swapping stories about what we had been doing since graduation. I was the only one who had done any traveling; the rest had gotten jobs and stayed around the hometown. The second night, we went to a softball game at one of the local parks and later to the Steak 'n Shake for a coke. While we were having our drinks, they told me they all had dates for the next night. I could see that my nights with my friends would be over for a while. I had been gone for almost three years and didn't know whom I could call for a date.

They told me to relax—they already had me fixed up. I asked if I knew the girl. They said no, and they didn't know her either. This bothered me a little. I wanted to know how they got me a date with a girl they didn't know. Don't worry, they said, their girlfriends knew two days ago that I would be coming along and had fixed me up with a blind date. If the girls had already asked someone to go on a blind date with me, I couldn't very well back out.

I asked for the girl's name and address, but none of them knew her name. "Don't worry about where she lives. We'll pick you up and take you when we pick up our girlfriends," they said. I was beginning to wonder what they were hiding from me. These guys could pull off some pretty good pranks, and I was hoping I wasn't about to be the main subject of one. There was also the fact that we were starting a date at eight o'clock, which seemed a little late. The last movie of the night usually started before eight.

My confusion ended when they explained that the girls we would be picking up were all students in the nursing program at Decatur and Macon County Hospital. It was a weeknight, and the girls had floor duty or study hours until eight o'clock. At eight, they were free to leave the campus but had to be back by ten when the dorm doors were locked. Two hours seemed like a pretty short time for a date, but I was assured they had everything planned out to fit the time schedule.

At seven thirty that next evening, three cars pulled up in front of my house and tooted their horns. I jumped in the first car with Carl Painter, a buddy I had ushered with at the Rogers Theater when I was in high school. He peeled away from the curb with the other two cars right behind him. I lived on the east side of town, and we had to get to the north side, where the hospital was located, before eight. We arrived with ten minutes to spare and waited for the girls.

Thirty seconds after eight, the front doors of the dormitory burst open, and a group of laughing girls emerged and headed our way. We all jumped out of the cars to greet them. After a brief introduction to the young lady who was to be my date for the evening, we loaded back in the cars and zoomed away. I had no idea where we were headed. This was not only a blind date: it was a mystery trip as well.

Carl wheeled the car into the parking lot of a small café, where we all piled out and rushed inside. I got the feeling this was something they had all done before. We ordered cokes. The frosty six-ounce bottles were delivered to our table with straw protruding from their tops. The coke in those six-ounce bottles disappeared in a hurry, and we once again rushed to the cars and roared off. My head was beginning to spin. Where were we rushing to this time?

I saw a road sign saying we were on US Route 51 and headed north. Not too far out of town, we turned onto a county blacktop headed west. The lights of the city were gone, and the black night of open country surrounded us. Sharp wedges of light coming from the headlights of the three cars cut through the darkness. Carl slowed our car, pulled off the blacktop, and turned out his lights. The other cars pulled in behind him.

Were they planning to stop here and make out with their girlfriends? What was I supposed to do? I didn't even remember my blind date's last name. I watched Carl. I expected to see him put his arm around his girl, but instead he started fiddling with the radio. Suddenly, the sound of the Glenn Miller Orchestra flooded the car with music. Carl turned the volume up to full and got out of the car. I heard the doors of the other cars open and the people spill out. By the time I had helped my date out of the car, the night air was filled with music. The radios in all three cars had been set on WSOY, the local station, which played big band music every night from eight to ten.

The shadowy shapes of dancing couples now filled the blacktop road. The only light came from the moon, the stars, and the glow from the radios in the cars.

It had been a warm day, and the heat from the asphalt could be felt through our shoes, but a gentle breeze kept the air above the blacktop comfortable. For half an hour, we danced to Benny Goodman, Tommy Dorsey, Les Brown, and Lawrence Welk. The time flew by much too fast, and it was suddenly time to rush the girls back to the dorm before the doors were locked. After a quick kiss and a promise that we would go out again in a couple of days, the girls ran giggling through the front doors.

It would be hard to find a lightly traveled blacktop road in this day and age. It's too bad that today's young people will miss the chance to dance to big band music on a blacktop road under the stars.

After Hours

~

Amy Lynch

After hours. That is such an alluring phrase. It conjures a moonlit picture, like an old home movie, in which I step out of the Northwestern Bell Telephone building in downtown Rapid City, South Dakota in the late 1970s. I walk out the door at midnight, and the street still holds some heat from the July day that I can feel through my sandals, but the air against my arms and legs is cool.

The corner is quiet. The other second-shift operators are still chatting and smoking upstairs in the break room, but they are long-timers with close friends. I'm the new girl, still in high school, with no one to chat with yet. I slip out first and look for my car. I parked it blocks away when I arrived for my 3 p.m. shift, but during the evening, my mom or dad will come downtown to move the car to a spot nearer the building, so I won't have to walk far at midnight. Safe inside it, I'm in no hurry to drive home. I sit and breathe and feel some of the tension of the job slide away as I watch the gaggle of other operators coming out the door, calling farewells over their shoulders and heading off to find their own cars.

After hours. Work is done, my parents are asleep at home, and I've nowhere particular to be. If I were a few years older, I might be tempted to go out for a drink, but sixteen is too young to buy a beer in South Dakota. Wound up and footloose, I drive home the long way, exploring the streets of my town by moonlight, where buildings and shadowed alleys are just rectangles of black and white.

I don't remember any particular stories from those hours, no sudden revelations or adolescent adventures, but that summer introduced me to a new state of mind, because I found some time that was all my own. As the youngest member of a close family, my life had been spent in orbit, and I was used to being steered by the activities and decisions of the people around me. At first, it was unsettling to realize that there was no one but me to decide how to spend those hours. Taking thirty extra minutes to drive home the long way caused no ripples. It was several weeks before I realized that after quietly unlocking the door and slipping into the house, I did not need to go right to bed. Gradually, I learned to relax into that expanded world and reveled in that freedom, even if my only exercise of it was to carry sandwiches to the backyard to nibble as I lay stretched out on the lawn watching the stars.

I remember that discovery of self-determination very fondly when I hear the phrase "after hours."

For the Love of Candy

~

Shelley Crouch

It was a damp and chilly night in late October. My youngest and I stood shivering along Main Street in Oblong, Illinois. We were there to watch my middle child play the drums with the junior high marching band in the annual Spooktacular parade. The streets were packed with spectators. I stood back near a storefront, huddled with other parents for warmth, while my second grader found a place on the edge of the road with the other kids, all hoping to pick up some candy.

The parade finally started. There were marching bands from all over the state playing their best pieces for the judges, and in between, local businesses with floats throwing loads of treats, but every time these goodies were tossed, the two kids next to mine would shove and push in front to get anything that landed nearby. These situations seem to encourage kids to be greedy. After this played out several times, my youngster turned to me, discouraged.

My mama bear instincts started to creep up, but I thought of the lesson I'd read that morning on loving our enemies. I said I was sorry those kids were acting that way, but I wanted to try something. I suggested to my seven-year-old to please give any candy caught to those boys. I promised we would buy a big bag of candy on the way home, but I suggested that we just treat those kids with extra kindness.

A thoughtful and generous person by nature, my child immediately took the advice to heart. The next time a candy bar was caught, it was offered directly to the others. They gave my kid a funny look and looked at each other as if it was a trick. They knew the kindness they were receiving was undeserved. Nevertheless, looking it over carefully, they took the offering. And my child kept giving them everything. It was a long parade with many entries, so my kid got a lot of loot, even standing next to these guys.

Eventually, and much to our mutual surprise, the most incredible thing happened. The boys started reciprocating, giving any candy they caught to my kid. Kindness had won. Enemies had become friends.

I wish I could end my story here, leaving you with good thoughts about the lessons we had learned that night. However, at the end of the parade, the last entry was the local Hershey factory from nearby Robinson. They were throwing full-size candy bars. I think I may have trampled three young children in my quest for the coveted Heath bar.

An Apology to Mr. Grech

~

Richard England

"The British! The English! It was their fault, you know. They don't teach you nothing at school. They occupied Malta for five years and the Luftwaffe bombed the hell out of us. So many people died—you have no idea. And for what? What did Malta have to do with anything? The British! Butchers!"

And then, silence for a moment. It's two in the morning in Bramalea, Ontario, and I'm riding shotgun in Charlie Grech's minivan. We're between jobs—Scotiabank and the furniture outlet — waiting at a stoplight at a deserted intersection. Outside, there's the hot summer night's shadowy terrain of empty used car lots and darkened strip malls. In the back, a couple of co-workers are staring idly out the window or drowsing. We've heard it all before. The light turns green; Charlie hits the gas, reaches down to the radio, the green light bringing his hand eerily out of night, as he turns up the volume again. I don't remember what synth-laden pop rock emerged; it was 1985, the wrong year for "War (What Is It Good For?)" or Nena's "99 Luftballons." Anti-war anthems were less common than the usual hymns to love (requited or un) and electronic celebrations of misery. We always listened to the same top forty station. In a night, we'd hear each song many times over.

There was enough irony, I suppose, in the fact that of all the minimum wage employees in all the suburbs in all the world, a lad named England had been hired by one who hated that nation and its people and blamed them for the suffering he'd likely endured as a small child when the Germans failed for years to expel the British navy and air force from a strategically valuable island in the Mediterranean. The British had clung on to that rock for years, despite devastating waves of destruction falling from the skies. I don't know any of those who died, but though he didn't mention names, I am pretty sure that Charlie did.

I was a pimply, immigrant Canadian teenager suffering through a freakish growth spurt that summer and the blinking representative of a despised occupying power. I'd gotten used to Charlie's occasional vehement history lessons, and the radio was so tediously repetitive that I didn't really mind.

I was too young to talk back and wouldn't have been able to muster the argument that seems obvious to me now. Someone would have occupied Malta during WWII, and the other side would have bombed it. I was a cleaner that summer. Charlie took his crew round to banks, stores, offices, and even a telephone exchange full of spooky, clacking shelves of circuitry. We started around seven at night and worked through 'til five or six in the morning. The first night, I had no idea the shifts were so long. Neither did my parents, and I was stunned to discover them on the sofa waiting for me, my mum bursting into tears as I stumbled in.

I'm not sure I learned much that summer: a little about waxing floors and cleaning bathrooms and a great deal about top forty '80s music, which I can still identify many years later, though the force of nostalgia has gradually overcome the contempt that overfamiliarity bred that summer.

I learned that I did not want to work nights again if I could help it, though I did, a little later in life. And I suppose I learned that however unpleasant or dull or tiring this little visit to the dark and dirty side of suburbia was, there were worse things—much worse. Charlie Grech, my first employer, on behalf of the English, the British, and the whole crew of Axis aerial warriors who rained down death from above—none of whom I ever met outside of movies or comic books—my apologies.

Hard Choices

~

Bill Heyduck

I was sixteen years old before the blissful white world I grew up in was shaken by my first encounter with racial prejudice. I was aware that all the people of color seemed to live in the same neighborhood, but I always thought it was by choice.

When I look back on my early years, I am amazed at how blind I was to all the racial divisions in my own high school. I lived in Decatur, Illinois, miles north of the Mason-Dixon Line. I thought racial prejudice was only in the south, but a look back at my old high school yearbook shows a different picture. The school choir was all white, as was the school band. There were only two high school clubs for those of color, and they were both for girls: the colored girls' chorus and the Crystal Bird Club.

I know the word colored isn't used today, but it is the word that was used when I was growing up in Decatur. The word negro was only used in National Geographic and scientific papers. The third, an ugly word, was sometimes used by people who somehow thought it made them look superior. I'm not sure why, but I'm uncomfortable calling someone black. Truthfully, I don't know any people who look black—brown, maybe. Then again, I don't know anyone who looks white. Pink would be more descriptive.

I grew up in a white/pink neighborhood and worked as an usher in a neighborhood movie theater. The theater drew its audience from the surrounding white/pink neighborhood. These small neighborhood theaters only got the chance to run the newer movies a few weeks after the first run movie houses downtown ran them. They also ran what were called "B" pictures with lesser-known actors.

This was in the 1940s, and movies operated a little differently back then. Lights did not come on at the end of each movie like they do today. Once the lights went out in the theater, they stayed out until the last showing at around eleven o'clock at night. Ushers, with their trusty flashlights, were needed to show customers to their seats after the theater darkened.

One busy Saturday night, two dark faces appeared in the line in front of the box office to buy tickets. In the year I had worked at the theater, these were the first colored people to come to a show. When the ticket seller spotted them, she sent the candy counter girl to get the manager. On entering the lobby, he saw why he had been summoned and went into action.

I didn't see any of this, but I heard about it later from the candy counter girl. My first knowledge that something was afoot was when I saw the theater manager rush up to the other usher, pointing to the interior of the theater as he talked. The other usher was still nodding his head when the manager whirled around and hurried over to me. "Do you have any seats left in the back row?" he whispered. I told him the back row in the side section was empty. "Good. Two colored people are on their way in, and if they come to you, put them in those back-row seats." With that said, he rushed back through the lobby and into his office.

The office door had just shut behind him when the couple entered the foyer and stopped. The man seemed to be asking the lady which aisle she wanted to sit in. My heart sank when she pointed at me, and they started in my direction. I gritted my teeth and cussed the manager under my breath. He had dumped his dirty little prejudice on me while he sat in his office guilt-free. I had never faced anything like this in my life.

The light was dim in the foyer, and it was only after they got closer that I saw the man was in uniform. I guess that was only natural, since it was 1944 and we were in the middle of World War II. By the time they reached my station, I could see he was wearing an infantryman's badge and two rows of ribbons on his chest. I had four uncles fighting in the war and from the look of those ribbons, I knew that man had been in the thick of it too. I took another look at the ribbons and then up into their smiling faces. I took a deep breath, put on my biggest smile, and said, "Where would you like to sit, sir?"

He said, "About halfway down would be fine."

I shone my flashlight on the floor behind me and marched down the aisle to the middle of the theater and stopped. "How's this?" I asked.

"This is fine, thank you."

I turned out my flashlight and started the long trip up the aisle. I felt good. I had done what I thought was right and was prepared to face the manager's wrath. To my surprise, the manager was nowhere in sight. He was still hiding in his office. I guess he thought that after giving his orders, he was finished with his dirty little job and could disappear. I don't know how he felt sitting alone in there, but I felt proud that I had followed my own principles and not supported his.

Didn't he know you can't tell a sixteen-year-old a damn thing and expect him to do it?

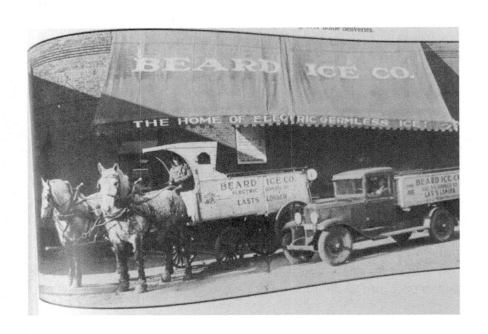

Some Men
I Liked in the '50s

~

Phyllis Bayles

I have a long history of buying milk. As far as I can remember, it all began with a wooden box right outside our back doorstep. Mother would put empty glass bottles in the box and the milkman would come, pick up them up, and replace the empties with full ones. It was always white whole milk. Mr. Milkman came at the same time every day, and Mother would be there waiting for him. She took the milk inside to the room off the kitchen and immediately put the bottles into the icebox. Sometimes she would leave him notes that said things like "Please leave two bottles of chocolate for the birthday party" or "We're going on vacation. We'll be gone for the next six days." Lots of times, she would leave him some kind of home-baked treat. I got to hand it to him, and he would give me a free small bottle of milk, shaking my hand and saying, "Thank you, Missy Phyllis!" to which I replied, "You're welcome Mr. Milkman."

One day, Mother took my hand, and we started walking up the alley. We were going to some new place called the "new Piggly

Wiggly." Pigs in Danville? At the end of the alley we reached the street, and I repeated the usual mantra "Use your eyes. Use your ears. And then use your feet." At the new Piggly Wiggly, I looked around. Where was the milk box? And there weren't any bottles! All I saw were some waxy cardboard carton things stacked up in a giant kind of icebox. Mother said it was a refrigerator. "Milk box" was a lot easier to spell.

After that, Mother would give me fifty cents and send me to the new Piggly Wiggly to buy a large carton of milk. I would walk home holding the paper bag with both hands. For me, it was a sad trip. First of all, it was a lot easier to just go out the back door, especially in the winter. And second of all, I never saw my friend Mr. Milkman again. Now nobody shook my hand when I bought milk. And nobody called me Missy Phyllis either!

Before the new Piggly Wiggly came into our neighborhood, Mother had an icebox. The ice truck would pull up, and my brother and I would run and grab chips off the back. Mr. Ice Man sat me on the front porch stoop and made up rhymes like "Ice is nice, but Philly is chilly."

Sometimes we would do what he called rhythm: "Stomp your feet while the ice you eat." He had a big hook called a pick that would hold a giant block of ice. He slung the ice over the blanket on his shoulder and carried it inside to put into the icebox. After the Piggly Wiggly came, Daddy bought Mother a new fridge. After that, I never saw Mr. Ice Man again.

One summer day, I was playing in the backyard, and I spotted something shining on the ground near the garden. It was a rock. But not just any dirty old yard rock. One whole side had a large chunk broken off. Inside the break, I saw shiny little purple rocks that sparkled in the sunlight.

Mother told me the rocks were called quartz. I put one in my pocket and headed for town to show my dad. On the way, I arrived at the chocolate shop owned by Mr. Georgie. He was Greek, and I couldn't pronounce his real last name. My dad was in business, and I'd often heard him talking about making trades with his vendors. Suddenly, I knew what to do. I pushed open the big glass door and went inside, where the air smelled delicious.

In the glass cases, I saw chocolate fudge, chocolate clusters with nuts, cream-filled chocolates, and chocolate topped with dried fruit. It was wonderful! Mr. Georgie, the candy man, was stirring a new batch of melted chocolate in a giant copper bin. "Look! Look!" I shouted. I took my treasure out of my dress pocket and proudly showed him my beautiful rock.

"Something that pretty is probably worth a lot of money!"

I gave Mr. Georgie my best and cutest smile. "Could I trade it for some chocolate?"

He did some thinking. Then he smiled and said, "Malista [yes]. Just go ahead and pick out one piece of chocolate candy that you like." I chose a chocolate peanut cluster and surrendered my precious rock. The deal was done!

I ate that piece of chocolate slowly, all the way home. It was so good, I wanted it to last forever. When I got home, I ran out to the backyard and started digging. The next day, I loaded up my wagon with rocks and went back to see Mr. Georgie. When he saw the wagon parked outside his front door, he stifled a gasp, but then he smiled and struck a deal with me: one rock a week until school started in September. I was in business as a rock vendor.

Years later, I went to the cemetery and laid a quartz rock on Mr. Georgie's headstone.

Seven days a week—yes, even on Sunday—Mr. Mailman came to our front porch. Usually, he just slipped the mail into the slot on the front door or left things on the porch, but Sundays were special. Every Sunday our comic books would come. They arrived in the afternoon after church. On comic book day, Mr. Mailman rang the doorbell. My brothers and I knew what that meant. We rushed to get my Little Lulu, Dean's Roy Rogers, and little Art's Mickey Mouse or Donald Duck.

Mr. Mailman would ask me to walk along with him to the next house and tell him about the stories in the comic book he had delivered the week before. As I look back on those walks, I realize that I was learning how to comprehend what I read.

One day, he told me that the post office was going to cease Sunday deliveries but that that would not change our comic book fun. I'd still see him six days every week, and one of them would definitely be comic book day.

On a cold winter day right after Christmas, Mother sat me down. She told me that my friend Mr. Mailman had died because his heart got sick. So I never saw him again. I guess I was getting too old for comic books anyway.

Gary lived three blocks away. He was our paper boy. He always walked jauntily along the sidewalks whistling a bunch of different tunes. As he walked, he folded the Danville Commercial-News into a rectangle, rolled it up, and tucked in the edges. It was really amazing. He could toss that paper onto a porch, and it would never break open. When he got to our house, I joined him for the rest of his paper route. We sang Broadway show tunes and songs from Your Hit Parade. I was very proud when he won a scholarship offered by the newspaper. He went on to get a PhD and became a well-loved professor at UCLA. Gary was only two years older than I was, and we were lifelong friends—that is, until the day I got a text: "Gary died today in Los Angeles."

Those days are gone. And so are those men, but my memories of them will always be with me. Back then, except for Gary, I didn't use their names. In my childish way, I simply thought of them as identified with their jobs. Times were different. Times were simpler. Work was different too, and because working men took time to be nice to kids, knowledge of the world came to us in different ways.

Those men who worked in our 1950s neighborhood are still tops among the men I have liked. Many of my favorite childhood moments were spent with them.

Summer

~

Donna Karbassioon

Pick a summer—any summer! One wasn't that much different from any other. It was always hot, and I always looked forward to those three months of glorious heat. If I had to pick a summer to remember, it would be the one when my father let me cut grass with his riding lawn mower. I started out cutting straight rows, but that was boring, so I decided to cut in a large circle and then continue to the center of the yard. When I was done, I thought it looked beautiful. My dad didn't have quite the same reaction.

It wasn't just cutting grass that I enjoyed. There were lightning bugs to catch. I used one of my mother's canning jars, poking holes in the lid. The light the bugs gave off was so exquisite, not iridescent or incandescent. It reminded me of the blinking lights at Christmas or even maybe the twinkling light of the stars.

At the top of my list of summer enjoyment was watching those stars with my dad while reclining on top of our picnic table. He was pretty savvy when it came to pointing out the different constellations in the sky. Some nights we had the special pass-by of the satellite Echo—or was it Sputnik? These fun nights return to me whenever I visit an observatory.

It wouldn't be summer without the occasional trip to the pool for swimming with friends. My other recollections are flooding in: riding my bike, and roller skating in the driveway. I have scars to prove it! On my birthdays, the ice cream was guaranteed to melt. Then there was swinging from the branches of the four giant willow trees—not ours, but some right at the edge of our property. My partner in crime was the boy who lived across the street. If you haven't already guessed, we played Tarzan and Jane.

As I'm writing this, here comes another fond memory, of cherry picking, and this time, the trees are ours. My grandmother made the best cherry pie. I was responsible for picking the cherries, since I was the only one who could climb to the top and beat the birds to their morning brunch. I was also the lucky one who had the lovely but messy task of pitting the cherries. No one is complaining here, because after all was said and done, the pie was so delicious, especially right out of the oven with some vanilla ice cream.

I also learned about bees that summer. A very large number of them settled in to make their hive in the next-door neighbor's tree. My dad asked if he could cut the branch so he could move them into a house he was going to make for them. The neighbor was delighted. It was beautiful. Their new home was like a penthouse condo. It was glass and wood—that way you could watch the activity of the bees. He built their new house on four stilts, just high enough to make it comfortable for viewing. The outfit he wore to capture the bees was so funny. He had a hat to which he added mosquito netting. He wore a long-sleeved shirt and gloves. The mornings were cool, and that proved to be the best moving time. I learned that bees are more lethargic when it is cool.

I could go on and on, but I think I'll take a rest and have a refreshing glass of homemade lemonade. Just one more thing— why does the water taste more delicious in the hot summer?

Anticipation

~

Amy Lynch

Children poised,

perched on chairs,

bodies leaning forward,

staring at bowls and saucers laden

with chalky Necco Wafers,

glossy M&Ms,

chubby gumdrops,

speckled nonpareils,

and mounds of plump white dinner mints,

waiting for the moment

when Poppy would press the last gingerbread timber into place

and they could reach out

to start the decoration.

Winter Daze: Memories of Snowy Days and Nights

~

Margie Checkley

When I think of winter, I recall so many great times outside when I was growing up. Oh, how I wish I could play in the snow again with the neighboring children. There were probably six or eight of us, all around the same age, who lived on our block.

We never knocked on any doors to ask them to come out and play: we just yelled their names in front of their house, and they would come running. We loved the beautiful big white snow that would fall and glisten under the intersection streetlight. This was our playground for winter sports. We never had any fancy equipment, just our ordinary and sometimes crazy imaginations.

We didn't even have a sled! My friends and I complained about this until one night we realized we had a small, old wooden rocker in the garage. Talk about excitement; this was it! We tied a belt to the bottom rung of the rocker and took turns pulling each other around on the new sled, which not only slid but rocked at the same time. There was rarely any traffic in the street, and the snow was packed perfectly for our adventure. What a magical time we had. After all those fun nights, we never thought about wanting a sled. We had the ultimate!

My favorite time during winter is dusk, when the snow is deep and glistening. There is something tranquil about walking in untouched, sparkling snow, just me and the silence. If I am lucky enough to enjoy the light of a full moon, I can almost shut out the world for a few minutes and enjoy the wonder of it all.

How can you not like winter just a little?!

4-H Style Show

~

Roxanne Frey

Everyone smiled as I stepped out on the stage. My confidence in my walk grew with each step. I turned to show the back of my 4-H skirt and heard laughter.

My last-minute trip to the bathroom had left the hem tucked into my waistband, revealing far more than I had planned.

Discerning the Sex
of a Kitten

~

Shelley Crouch

Four-year-old Dustin had one of his friends over, and they were playing with our new baby kittens. Dustin told his friend, "This one is Fred."

His friend asked him, "How do you know it's a boy?"

"It's easy," Dustin exclaimed. "Just turn it over and look at its feet! That's what my dad does!"

My Baby Brother

~

Hannah Eads

It was a sunny October day. I was almost four. My brother John and I were told to play outside. The front door opened, and Dr. Hoff emerged.

"You have a new baby brother," he said.

"Where did he come from?" I asked.

"I found him in the corn field."

I didn't know doctors fibbed!

Magical Thinking

~

Amy Lynch

I enjoyed my childhood and all of its magical trappings: the stories before bed, camp songs on car trips, Halloween costumes, and visits by the Tooth Fairy and the Easter Bunny. My pleasure in those things just changed sides when I had kids.

Now I got to read the bedtime stories, swap quarters for teeth under pillows, fill stockings, and hide the Easter eggs while the kids were asleep. Making that magic come alive in our house filled me with joy.

It all seemed odd to Doug. He knew who Santa, the Tooth Fairy and the Easter Bunny were, but he couldn't remember a time in his life when he'd believed in any of them. However, he saw my pleasure, and he could tell our kids enjoyed it, so he avoided spilling the beans while they were young.

Erin, however, was her father's daughter, and she struggled to mesh the magical stories with her growing understanding of the world. Even when she was two, the mechanism of Santa's sleigh seemed so unlikely that she thought it had to be a mistake. This careful analysis of the details continued to be her style, and at five, she announced a well-thought-out theory to explain how the Easter

Bunny traveled so far and with such an enormous load on a single night. She told me she'd been thinking about it, and she suspected that the Easter Bunny wasn't really a 'normal' bunny. She thought there was probably another planet, like Earth, but where the people were bunnies. They'd probably invented space travel and every year they sent one or more of their fastest bunnies to come and deliver baskets, but whenever anyone on Earth saw them, they thought they were seeing just a regular bunny. "Well maybe," I replied.

Finally, at age six, she challenged me directly and asked, "Is there really a Santa?"

Faced with the blunt question and knowing Doug had never been at ease with this deception—I hesitated. She read my face, and suddenly her own crumpled. She ran upstairs and into her room. I followed her up the steep stairs and found her face down on her bed sobbing. When I sat down beside her, she turned her face to me and choked out the terrible conclusions she had reached: "There is no Santa. And there-there-there isn't an Easter Bunny either, and y-y-y-y-*you* are the Tooth Fairy!"

Erin crashed back into her pillow, weeping. I rubbed her back, murmuring, until she quieted. After a few moments, she sat up with a look of fierce determination on her face.

"Kyle must not find out. We need to make sure he never finds out."

You see, Erin was my daughter too, not just Doug's, and while she couldn't persuade her logical mind to believe in the magic, she still loved the idea and wanted Kyle to have it. Poor Kyle was so well shielded that he may have been ten years old before he discovered the awful truth about Santa at school.

We weren't ever going to tell.

My Mother's Wisdom

~

Julie Rea

I was an army brat in the 1950s, and when my father was stationed near Stuttgart, Germany, I spent my time making new friends, becoming accustomed to American army schools, and reading a lot. In the middle of many life changes, reading seemed the most relevant thing to do, I guess. After all, I was still ten, a bit confused and trying to settle into a new life.

I had devoured *Florence Nightingale* by Laura Richards a few short days after my eleventh birthday when the decision came to me, suddenly, to be a nurse when I grew up. I could clearly see myself in a long skirt, carrying a softly glowing lantern among wounded soldiers on a Crimean battlefield. By the end of the book, I was convinced that I could nurse any type of wound and offer comfort to a man slowly leaving this world with my hand resting gently on his forehead. Looking back, I think the long skirt and softly glowing lantern were the magic touches.

With Nurse Nightingale's passion for her life's mission echoing deep in my eleven-year-old heart, I followed, page after page, her compassion and bravery during sleepless nights among the wounded and dying. I shared my dreams for the future with my mother, who assured me that nursing was a fine career to consider.

A year or so later, there was an incident in our fourth-floor walk-up that changed the presumed course of my life in less than a minute. I remember most vividly that my mother and sister and I were in our brightly lit kitchen when Bruno, our German Shepard–mix dog, entered the room after being outside for his nightly run. He was his usual self, greeting each of us in turn, when he stopped suddenly and, as they say in the medical world, lost his cookies.

One glance at what he left on my mother's kitchen floor sent me, at the speed of light, to the family bathroom. My mother's words, her voice raised and following me very fast, were every bit as inspired and purposeful as any I had read in *Florence Nightingale*: "If you're going to throw up when the dog does, Julie Ann, you can forget nursing!"

To this day, I can hear Mama's words, the tone of her voice, and the certainty of her wisdom. Never again have I given one single thought to pursuing a nursing career. Mind you, I did retire several years ago from a satisfying career as a licensed medical social worker. For years, I served happily alongside many nurses, and I continue to appreciate their fortitude and bravery in doing what my mother wisely knew I was not suited for.

Last Breath of Summer

~

Lois Dickenson

My big toe is sticking through a hole in my Keds. I concentrate on that new hole as I hitch a leg over the rough wooden side of the corn hiker. I need the distraction. This dare is a really scary one. I fit my small shoes, first the holey one, then the other, snugly down on the narrow conveyor slat. A few laggard corn kernels skitter under my light weight. With both feet turned outward, I lean over and grab the sides of the chute. They're an awkward width apart, forcing my back into an uncomfortable arch and my arms to spread out like the chickens' wings when the hens squawk-fight in the barnyard.

I try not to gulp a breath of air. My brother did this, I tell myself, and my sister too. It's my turn. It doesn't matter that they are both years older and inches taller than me. The dare has been given and must be taken up. I eye the greasy chain that runs in a shallow groove in the hiker's floor. If I step in any of that grease, I'll slide down the chute for sure.

That narrow length of the chute rises before me, angling up, up, and up some more to the dome in the roof of the grain bin. After one quick glance, I look doggedly at the bit of the floor in

49

front of me. I take a deep breath. Tuning out my brother's scoffing voice, I begin to climb. One foot up, then the next foot. My arms ache already from their awkward positioning. I wish I could grab the carry slats, then run up the center of the hiker instead of the sides.

Can't do that. It's too skinny to get a good grip, I think.

Another foot up, setting it firmly, before moving the next.

It's no different from climbing the big maple tree. I climb that tree nearly every day. Mom says I'd live in it if could.

I really like my maple tree. My sisters prefer the weeping willow that grows at the corner of the front ditch and the driveway. It does have easier handholds and a big space in the middle of all the fronds that makes a good hidey-hole. But my maple has big fat limbs that I can stretch out on and dream or watch birds or clouds on hot summer afternoons.

One foot up, next foot up.

I've been climbing a long time, seems like. I wonder how far?

I look down, which is a mistake. Dizzily, I brace my feet and cling to the sides of the hiker shell. I'm a lot higher up than my favorite tree limb. Shaky but determined, I focus on the next step to take and move my foot up to the next slat. More loose corn skitters under my foot. I move the next foot, then the next, again and again, over and over.

One foot, two foot, I chant in my head. Don't stop, next foot. I try not to think about how high off the ground I am. In my jabbering head, a random thought floats to the surface: Dad's going to kill me if he finds out about this.

That would be after Mom has her go at tanning my backside, but good. She'd use something worse than the usual flyswatter, for sure. I wonder if Dad will whup my brother worse than me, just for egging me on. Probably so.

One foot, two foot, don't stop, next foot. I try to distract myself from the growing scaredy-cat tightness in my chest. My new teacher—I grab at that thought. She's very pretty and glossy, but I don't like her. She seems mean, but not the paddling kind of mean. Writing all our names on the blackboard with our weekly quiz scores...that just isn't fair. And did she have to write the three lowest scores in red chalk and put big stars by the three highest scores? She says it will help us do our best, but it just hurts our feelings, I think. She has a thin kind of smile, too. I don't think she really likes kids. It's been two weeks already, and I don't think I can trust her at all.

I wish I had Miss Grace again this year. She's like Grandma, all kind and twinkly.

One foot, two foot, don't stop, next foot.

I grab another stray thought for distraction. Mike, my friend Mike. He's started acting a bit weird. I've known him a long time—since kindergarten. His name nearly always follows mine on the class list, so we always end up sitting near each other. Lately, he's started teasing me, tagging me on the playground, or egging the other boys to do it. Maybe it's because his name is in red on the blackboard pretty often. Not sure why that makes him come after me, though. It's not as if my name is followed by a star that often. Maybe I should start ignoring him the way Christy and her friends ignore the boys, although they can be kind of mean. No...I'll just tell Mike to cut it out. That will make me feel OK about it, and maybe it'll work.

One foot, two foot....

Where is the top? I've been climbing forever!

My back hurts from being bent at this odd angle for so long. I need to stand up and stretch in the worst way. My right foot slips a little on some loose corn, and I clutch the rough wood 'til my fingers turn white. My brother is yelling something from down below, but I can't make it out. I can't quit now; he'll never let me forget it if I do. I edge up another step. The carrying slats are spaced just far enough apart to make each step up uncomfortably wide. A dull ache starts in my calves and thighs. I catch a glimpse of metal out of the corner of my eye. Two more aching steps and a pewter-colored expanse arches away, cutting into a blue sky.

One foot, two foot...and again, and again. Now there is nothing but gray metal beside and below me. I don't dare to look up from the hiker's floor. Taking a chance, I reach out to fumble for the roof dome. I must be close. Please, Lord, let it be there. My fingers grope for a few terrifying moments before latching onto a vent opening. I clutch the sun-warmed metal tightly and pause to breathe for a few moments. Slowly, I straighten up and look out over the landscape.

Dazzled and amazed, I look out over my own home ground, all brown and golden and green but rendered wholly new by my lofty perspective. Far off to the east I can see the Stafford farm with its wading stream, and beyond that, the line of the Osage orange trees that shade the road all the way down to the village of Vermilion. To the north, the flat prairie stretches endlessly, 'til land and sky blend seamlessly, a mosaic of gray harvested soy fields and golden-brown ones filled with dying corn stalks. And there, to the west, that's the grove of black walnut trees that we harvest sometimes. A little beyond, Uncle Phil's big barn shimmers just on the horizon. Our road runs in straight lengths and subtle curves with the land until it too disappears into the horizon.

Cautiously, I tilt my head back, just a little. The bright blue September sky, newly deep and mysterious, seems just a finger's touch away. This is better than my maple tree, scarier, but this view touches my dreamer's soul profoundly. Victorious, I take a long breath, filling my lungs with the dusty scents of ripe grain and dry earth, a last heady breath of this dying summer.

Home

~

Marty Gabriel

Headless bunnies disturb the snow

where their silence did not protect them.
Better to have been neither heard nor seen.

Inside, where God has taken flight
and Kennedy inspires hope,
we little ones take note

and await the coming of Limbaugh
and Monty Python.

Once, I Was Eight

~

Yoana Yordanova

I believe Littlest Pet Shop was my greatest obsession when I was eight years old. It all started when my friend got a toy. Well, if my friend had it, then of course I wanted it too! So the next time I went to the store, I picked out the cutest little bunny toy and named her Cupcake. It didn't stop there. I bought more LPSes, as I called them, and soon enough, I had an army of doe-eyed toys in my room. There was a small space near my closet that was specially designated for this army. Sometimes I'd lie on the floor and stare at my toys in their little plastic houses; it was as if I was in their world. My friend and I would play for hours, imagining our little friends going to balls and meeting handsome strangers. I suppose we were trying to imagine what it would be like when we were older.

Years passed by, and we still held LPSes close to our hearts. But at eleven, I moved away. I packed up my darling toys, and we started a twelve-hour journey to Illinois, our new home. In a couple of months, everything was unpacked and arranged in my room. Everything but my darling toys. I had forgotten all about them. I walked over to the big blue box that contained them and was about to open the lid. My hand lingered, then drew away. I stood there until my mom suddenly called me for dinner.

I cast a last glance at the blue box and just walked away.

The Substitute and Sam

~

Hannah Eads

He walked around the classroom with measured steps, holding a yardstick in his hand, hoping that it would establish order. He watched the students as they arrived and took their seats, his stern expression giving notice that he would not put up with any nonsense. Mr. Newgent was a young man of small stature with a head of thick brown hair and piercing brown eyes. He wore a brown suit with a starched white shirt and a black bow tie, much like a typical schoolmaster of the early 1920s.

The Conlogue School was a white-frame, one-room country school located on a gravel road at Bell Ridge, north of Route 16 in Edgar County, Illinois. There was an outhouse several yards behind the building. A pile of chopped wood was stacked at the back door for making a fire in the potbellied stove. A pump near the back door had a tin cup hanging from it, and there was a swing set at the corner of the dirt playground. At recess, the boys often played marbles, while the girls jumped rope or played hopscotch. All the pupils liked to join in games of tag.

Mr. Newgent drove to the school in his Model T from his home in Brocton, several miles northwest of the school. He arrived early, so he didn't see any of the students as they walked to school from their farms. As they filed in on this clear spring morning, they wondered to themselves, "Where is Mrs. Culver?" She was never absent from her teaching duties.

One of the older students, Sam, had picked up a small striped garter snake that he found wriggling along the side of the road as he trudged to school that morning. He had planned to place it in Mrs. Culver's desk drawer just to see her reaction. But now he didn't have a chance as he scurried to his seat under the watchful gaze of the substitute.

The class stood to recite the pledge of allegiance, and he could feel the snake nestling in the front pocket of his bib overalls. Later, as the class was busy with their lessons, Sam squirmed in his seat, hoping he could let the snake out on the playground at recess.

Mrs. Culver would probably have made him stand in the corner, but he could only imagine what his punishment might be if the snake got out—a whack with that yardstick or worse!

The older students helped the younger ones with their lessons as Mr. Newgent paced around the room. That morning seemed like an eternity until he rang the bell for recess. Sam ran as fast as he could onto the playground, where the loosed snake slithered away in the bushes. None of the students had ratted on him, and he had escaped punishment!

The next morning, the class clapped and let out a collective sigh of relief as they took their seats and saw that Mrs. Culver was back. They told her they had been terrified of the substitute, fearing a whack on their knuckles from his yardstick. Sam, the freckle-faced class mischief-maker, was especially glad to see Mrs. Culver. And this time, there was no snake in his pocket!

Author's note: This story was told to me by my aunt, Kate Culver, about my father, Gordon Newgent.

The Egg Thief

~

Lois Dickenson

I don't like chickens. They are silly, witless creatures, both noisy and messy. I should know. We've raised hundreds and hundreds of them on our farm just during my short lifetime. Eggs and meat and the steady weekly income from the local hatchery are the only things that make keeping them worthwhile, and in my mind it's a close call. My dad thinks otherwise, though, so we keep chickens.

It's because of the chickens that I'm out here tramping through the dusk of late October. In the mysterious alchemy of family dynamics, the chore of evening chicken duty was transferred from my older sister to me last summer. Mary doesn't like the chickens any more than I do, so I suspect she had a hand in the transfer. At eight-almost-nine, I was deemed old enough to carry baskets of eggs safely down an unpaved lane and through our backyard—littered with low-hanging branches, clotheslines, tree roots, and the occasional toy—after dark, by flashlight. Lucky me.

Mary explained the whole deal to me last summer, and really it didn't seem that hard. Just add chicken meal to the feeders, top off the water, gather the last of the day's eggs, and chase down any of the birds too stupid or stubborn to come into the chicken house after dark. Easy-peasy.

Mmm…yes and no. The food and water bits are easy enough. Chasing down strays is a bit tougher, especially with the nights falling earlier and earlier. Speaking of which…yep, there they are, a trio of semi-escapees hiding in the underbrush on the south side of the chicken yard. Rather, trying to hide in the underbrush, I should say. All our chickens are industrial-grade pure-white hens, so they practically glow in the dark. With a near-full moon tonight, they are sure to be dinner for any passing stray dog or coyote. They can't even get to the safety of the low tree branches across the fence, since they are terrible fliers. I set the egg basket down by the henhouse door and reach in to turn on the lights. Hopefully, the lighted door will give the strays a target in the dark. Chicken-shooing time!

Herding chickens is not difficult. It involves a great deal of hand-waving, wing-flapping, generalized squawking, the occasional small pebble, and the ability to lunge quickly to one side or the other to keep the troops in order. I've been doing it for years, although not usually by moonlight. No matter. In just a few minutes, I manage to nudge the last of the truants into the coop.

Water next. I open the stopcock on the rain barrel to let fresh water flow into the trough leading into the henhouse. It doesn't take much. I turn off the water and reach over to get a scoop of feed from the storage bin. Armed with food and my egg basket, I face my least favorite part of my job—gathering eggs.

I don't like chickens. They don't like me either, which seems only fair. Mary was full of useful advice when she turned this job over to me. Be as quiet as you can. Watch where you step: there are often eggs on the floor. Don't linger under the rafter beams because roosting chickens will do…what roosting chickens do with a splat. There's a knack to winkling eggs out from under a laying hen—just be soft, slow, and quiet.

I do not have the winkling knack, even after these past four months. Hen pecks hurt, and I rarely make it out without four or five to show. They gain me no sympathy from anybody, so I never mention them anymore. Work gloves would help, but they don't come in child sizes, and fresh, smooth eggs can be slippery.

Okay, I tell myself, time to get on with it. Take a deep breath first—large chicken houses, no matter how clean, have a lingering acrid odor. I push through the door into the dim light of the henhouse. Occupied with the feed scoop and egg basket, it takes me a few seconds to realize something odd is going on. It is awfully quiet—and large groups of chickens are never very quiet. There are no chickens rooting around on the floor either, like they always do. Puzzled, I swing my flashlight round, and there they all are: in the nesting boxes, on top of the nesting boxes, up in the rafters, all as high up as they can get. They don't seem particularly alarmed, though. I suppose it must be some kind of weird bird thing going on. I give a mental shrug and turn to top off the chicken feeding trough ...

And I freeze. Red eyes glare from the back end of the feeder...red eyes above a long narrow snout gaping open to show sharp pointed teeth, a fat white body behind with a whipping, naked pink rat tail. Ugh, ugh, *ugh*!

Now, with five active kids who were outdoors more often than not, the family rules regarding wild animals are clear. Don't poke at snakes with a stick. Don't dig up vole tunnels or ground wasp nests. Don't throw stuff at the bats in the old haymow to wake them up. Don't try to catch bunny rabbits or fox kits or baby skunks. Don't pet stray dogs, cats, or raccoons. To sum up: leave the wild things alone and they'll leave you alone.

All that is well and good, but this situation is different. That red-eyed rat thing has invaded people territory—well, chicken territory, but the chickens are ours, so it's the same thing. I center the flashlight beam on the feeder again to get a better look at the intruder. Instead of one pair of red eyes, there are now about ten eyes, all staring straight at me. Big Mama Possum lets out a warning hiss. Backing away suddenly seems like a very good idea.

Possums...what do I know about possums? I've glimpsed them before from time to time, but not often. Could I just go about my egg-gathering business and let her be? Probably not, I decide. Aren't possums like raccoons in that they eat anything? She's obviously been eating the chicken feed up to now, but with young ones in tow, who knows what she'll go after next? The eggs, of course, and maybe even the hens themselves. Nope—she has to come out of here, and it is too big a job for me. I back out of the henhouse and latch the door as quietly as I can, then take off through the twilight at a trot.

"Dad! Dad!"

I burst onto the back porch, empty egg basket in hand and a little out of breath. Dad, seated as his usual spot at the kitchen table, looks up from the book he was reading. He looks at the empty basket and my mucky boots, which stops me at the kitchen door.

"There's a possum in with the chickens and she has babies and she hissed at me, and the hens are all quiet and—"

Dad doesn't quibble. "Bob! Get your heavy jacket and work gloves. Don't forget your boots, either." He is already past me on the porch, pulling on his own jacket. My brother pushes past me and looks at Dad.

"Possum in the chicken house."

Bob mutters something under his breath. Like me, Bob is not fond of chickens, and at age eleven, he can get away with muttering a bit. Geared up, Bob and I follow Dad out to our pickup. Dad throws some empty feed sacks in the back. I know then that a possum, even one in the henhouse, doesn't merit getting Dad's varmint gun from the basement. Dad never likes to kill wild things unless he has to.

Back at the chicken house door, Bob and I get our marching orders. Bob is to make a lot of noise in the coop, both yelling and banging on the lid of the feed barrel. Dad will do the possum grabbing. My job is to stay outside and out of the way. I am both relieved and a little disappointed to miss all the upcoming excitement. I'm sure I can make as much noise as Bob. But then again, I don't want to end up with a scared possum in my lap either. Staying out of the way suddenly seems about right.

As I wait at the door, Bob launches into a veritable opera of noise. Howling wildly, yelling (sometimes using words I'm not supposed to know) at top volume, he bangs the metal lid against anything within reach. Dull thuds mean he's hitting the support posts or nesting boxes, but that metal clang has to be him hitting the metal feeder itself. Squawking, flapping chickens add a grand, if panicked, element to all the uproar.   "Got her!" Dad's voice cuts through the racket.

The uproar fades to just the agitated cries of the hens, which don't quite cover the noise of Dad bagging up one—or rather six—possums. Bob comes grinning through the door and replaces the lid on the feed barrel. He gives me a little victory punch on the arm. "Should've seen her go all stiff! It was great!"

Dad comes out carrying a feed sack knotted at one end. Nothing is moving inside, and it reeks like two day-old roadkill. Dead, maybe, but little squeaking noises show the babies are alive at least. I open my mouth to ask, but Bob's still going on about his victory.

"Never seen a possum 'play possum' before, Dad! I scared her right into it, didn't I?"

"Yeah. Good job, son." Dad reaches down and ruffles the back of my head, which I'm too old for but don't mind too much. "You too, punkin." He drops the feed sack in the back of the truck and hands me down my egg basket. "Better finish up. School tomorrow."

I watch as the pickup drives down the lane and turns onto the road, heading east toward Baber's woods. I know then that Mama Possum will be ok, despite the stink she gave off in the sack. Good job, indeed. I turn back to the henhouse. Time to finish this job, too.

An Unlikely Poetry Reading

~

Bob Clapp

At twelve noon sharp, five carpenters unfastened their tool belts and dropped them on the unfinished floor. It was dinner time, so they gathered their lunch boxes from their trucks and sat in a circle, some on the floor and some on five-gallon buckets of drywall compound. As they drew out their cheese and bologna sandwiches, one member of that noble gathering produced a brown, faded, and dog-eared book of poems by nineteenth-century masters.

Stan, my oldest sibling and the elder among us, began reading aloud one of his favorites:

"Maud Muller on a summer's day.
Raked the meadow sweet with hay."

We listened intently, following the tale of almost-blossoming love between a judge on horseback and the suntanned Maud. It was a love that never came to fruition, and we all felt dismayed as Stan approached the end:

"For of all sad words of tongue or pen,

The saddest are these: 'It might have been!'"

That poem was a favorite of Stan's, along with another by the nineteenth-century master John Greenleaf Whittier, "The Barefoot Boy."

Stan passed the book to our youngest brother Dale, who flipped through the pages until he found his own favorite, Henry Wadsworth Longfellow's "A Psalm of Life." Listening as Dale read, we embraced the challenges issued by him and Longfellow:

"Let us be up and doing
With a heart for any fate
Still achieving, still pursuing
Learn to labor and to wait."

It wasn't a usual scene for poetry readers. You might expect such activity in the halls of a university or at some civic center — not on a dusty jobsite where a bunch of rough-cut carpenters had paused for lunch. The book came to me next, and I laid aside my unfinished sandwich to search for one of my favorites, James Russell Lowell's "The Present Crisis." He wrote it in the nineteenth century to confront the evils of slavery, and I could easily quote many lines from memory:

"When a deed is done for Freedom, through the broad earth's aching breast,
Runs a thrill of joy prophetic, running on from east to west,
And the slave, where'er he cowers, feels the soul within him climb
To the awful verge of manhood, as the energy sublime
Of a century bursts full blossomed on the thorny branch of Time."

Later, during the long afternoon hours of labor, one could hear phrases and sentences from these poems being quoted above the din of power saws and the banging of hammers:

"... time makes ancient good uncouth,
They must upward still, and onward who would keep abreast of Truth" or

"Tell me not in mournful numbers
Life is but an empty dream!"

Where that little brown book has gone, I don't know. Perhaps it is in the library of one of my brothers. It really doesn't matter. I will always cherish the memory of those five rough young carpenters sharing their favorite poems over lunch. Many of the lines have burned their way into my heart, and I repeat them to this day.

"What is so rare as a day in June?
Then, if ever, come perfect days ...."

Over the years, I have watched for those perfect days and seen many of them. This June, there have not been many so far — too hot, too wet, too windy — but I can think of two. On both of them, I went fishing with good friends. I took Steve to the big Embarras where we caught nearly two dozen fish. On another perfect day, Stan and I caught a dozen sunfish in the Oakland Lake.

Those were perfect June days not because of their mild temperatures or soft winds but because they were shared in fellowship with good friends. At Oakland, I gave away one of my treasured fishing poles to a young man who told us he had broken his and didn't have the money to buy a new one. That made my day, and his, even more perfect- even though he was not a "barefoot boy with cheek of tan" or "turned up pantaloons"!

Providential Grace

~

Rayma Laughlin

Spiritual awakenings, often movements or revivals, are a rich part of America's history. For example, the Great Awakening, the wave of fervor to abandon dying practices and rituals, began in eighteenth-century Scotland and England and then made its way to the colonies. As significant as these larger movements are, it's important to remember the effect that even one person can have on another, leading them to God, especially in times of crisis.

Such was the case for my husband, Jim, after his father's open-heart surgery in 1997. Grandpa seemed to be recovering and almost ready to leave the hospital when he passed out while attempting to stand by his bed. Something had gotten into his lungs, and a routine recovery became a very different experience. This crisis seemed to have presented an opportunity which awakened the priest in my husband as he ministered to his father so powerfully and lovingly.

What makes this story even more remarkable is the background of Jim's relationship with his parents. Critical attitudes and resulting hurt and ill will had been at work in family relationships well before my husband's generation. By Grandpa's seventy-ninth year, it had been especially hurtful for my husband that his parents seemed to take so little interest in our children's activities, such as athletic events, especially since my parents were very present in our family's lives. One time, my father even came to a baseball game after receiving a chemotherapy treatment that very day.

During those three weeks that Jim's father fought for his life after his dramatic setback, something came alive in my husband's spirit, readying him for the unanticipated moment that arose. His mother and sister had been fairly constant in their hospital visiting, and my husband was generally inhibited in their presence. However, after Grandpa's setback, something fortuitous happened. Jim had been called at school about his father's changed condition and felt compelled to go to the hospital before the end of the school day. When he arrived, surprisingly, he found his father alone and about to have a tube put down his throat, which would hinder his ability to speak. Jim took that small but significant piece of time to encourage his father in matters of faith. Grandpa had been estranged from his brother; now Jim presented the need to forgive that brother and get right with God. Jim also shared his own faith in those few but eventful minutes, and his father responded favorably to it all. Then the tube was inserted, something his mother had not anticipated when she and her daughter left to go home for lunch.

By the time they returned, Grandpa was on a ventilator, and Jim had ministered a much-needed conversation about faith and forgiveness. I believe that because Jim was so selflessly the God-ordained priest his father needed, Jim's own hurt and disappointment of many years were washed away by the Holy Spirit. Jim was never bothered by past events again, truly experiencing the peace of God. The next few weeks, he was with his father at night, talking about times in the past and playing some music, including Jesuit songs on an old tape player. His mom and sister would cover the days, unaware of the meaningful exchange between father and son until after Grandpa died.

Although there were times of hope, Grandpa lost the struggle to recover. I think the crucial minutes before the tube went in were the only time Jim pointedly and personally spoke to his dad about matters of faith. He was a kind, loving, and attentive son, wonderfully enabled to do so much good when his father needed it the most by the great grace of God. I cannot think of another time when Jim experienced an awakening of the presence of God within him to such an extent, giving him a holy boldness at a critical moment before his father's death. It still impresses me that Jim was the one to get those last few minutes of conversation with his father. Surely it was the outpouring of God's grace and the awakening it stirred up in Jim that changed the course of both of their lives eternally.

Hometown
~
Jane Gilbert

I grew up in Charleston in the 1940s. I liked it here. I knew the neighbors, had friends, could walk or ride my bike anywhere I wanted to go, felt safe. But I had a father who wanted me to have a broader perspective on the world, so I got to travel and see that not everywhere was like Charleston. When we visited relatives in Chicago, I was taken to museums, to the Art Institute, to the theater or the ballet, things unavailable at home. By the time I reached junior high, I had begun to think that my hometown was a pretty ho-hum place and anywhere else would be much more interesting.

This was only reinforced by the arrival at my high school of a new, young language teacher from the East with a brand-new master's degree from Harvard. She thought she had come to the Wild West to civilize us and made no secret of it. I adored her, took all her classes, and hung out in her room after school. She gave me reading lists of the classics, which I devoured, and talked about the cultural life in Boston and New York. She was what I wanted to become. I was embarrassed to be from such a small hick town. When I left at age eighteen to go to college, I vowed to myself that I would never, ever live in Charleston again.

After college, I did spend a year and a half in New York City, an experience I wouldn't have missed but would not want to repeat. I also lived in four other states, finally landing in the Chicago area for the last twenty-five years of my career. All that time, I kept coming back to Charleston to visit as my parents got older. I could see that the town had grown and changed as the university grew and the center of commerce shifted from the Square to Lincoln Avenue. It was interesting to watch as an outside observer, but I had no emotional ties here beyond my parents. My high school had closed, and none of my classmates lived here anymore either.

Then came retirement, and my husband and I were ready to get out of the suburbs. We talked about various university towns around the country, or perhaps the mountains of North Carolina. But at the same time, my parents needed us as one old-age crisis after another started piling up. What if we moved to Charleston to be on hand and help out? It would be temporary, of course. Move there, stay just as long as we were needed, and then go find our retirement dream.

It all went so smoothly. The perfect house appeared almost out of nowhere. We were welcomed by people we didn't know but who knew about us. We found a church that was a fit and made friends quickly. And the biggest surprise of all—my husband, who had never lived in a town smaller than Decatur, liked it very much. Three years later, when we could have left, we had put down roots. We were staying.

Twenty-five more years have gone by, and I'm still here. I know my neighbors, I have lots of friends, and I feel safe—or as safe as anyone can be in this crazy age. I may not walk or ride a bike as much as seventy years ago, but I can drive anywhere I need to go in ten minutes. There are fine medical services here, many cultural events available locally, and much more available electronically. True, there are days when I would kill for a really first-rate grocery store, but then I remember the crowds, the traffic, the isolation of metropolitan living. I was wrong when I was eighteen. Charleston is a good place to live, and I have come home.

A postscript: And then came the pandemic. Once again, the pull of family ties proved stronger than a geographical preference. Just as I never expected to move back to Charleston, I never expected to move away again, but it is good to be with family during these difficult days. I've always considered Minnesota my home away from home. Little did I know that it would one day *be* my home. I miss Charleston.

Mack, Mary Lincoln, and Me

~

Stacy Lynn

Mary Lincoln is next to me at the front of the room, and behind me is her white-frosted 196th birthday cake. People, mostly friendly-faced retirees, slowly file into the conference center of the Lincoln Home in Springfield, Illinois. Unwinding themselves from scarves and coats, they greet each other and seat themselves in molded plastic chairs lined up in careful rows. I breathe in the smell of the cold, which has wafted into the room upon their coats and gray hair, mingling with the smell of wool and coffee. Several people keep their coats on, and some hunch their chins into their collars.

If the room is cold, its chill is lost on me. I am sweaty with nerves and menopause and grief. I envy them their swaddling and long to grab a large, over-frosted corner of that cake and escape this hot room. I want to run away from these bundled-up people who have assembled on a freezing-cold December evening to see Mrs. Lincoln and to hear about my forthcoming biography of her life.

Mary Lincoln greets a friend, and the hooped skirts of both women rustle. The crinkling of fabric and the chatter of friendship snaps me out of my fixation on the temperature of the room. I am blasted out of my daydream of eating a stolen piece of that cake in my own home, alone in bed. I am reminded of the reality of my unhappy presence here. Mrs. Lincoln, her friend, and all of these people have come for a birthday party, but although there is such good feeling and warm communion in this room, I am silent and still. I am apart from these people and not of this world. I am here out of an obligation made before my life fell into ruin, and I am in no shape for celebration.

"What in the hell am I doing here?" I whisper to Kevin.

"You've done this a hundred times," he says. "You'll be great."

My husband has always said this to me before a speech or presentation, the utterance of it so mindless there is no time for him to reconsider it. The muscle memory of his tongue doesn't allow him to pause and remember that this time is different. I am different. The world is different. I do not blame him for it, because I remember the meaning of the words when he used to say them, their power a balm to my public-speaking jitters. But this is not typical pre-lecture nerves. This is a grieving husk of my former self trying to do something I no longer have the mental and emotional capacity to do. This is one of those terrible after-Mack firsts, and my heart tenses at the sorrow of it. I cannot even remember writing my biography of Mary Lincoln, and now I am supposed to talk about it in front of an audience? They expect me to form words and to shape sentences when even my capacity for reading novels has been given up to grief?

"I cannot do this," I whisper to myself and to no one.

I spy a lonely chair away from the traffic of the assembling people. I place my coat and bag upon the chair and turn to face the wall, pretending to consult my notes. Squeezing my eyes against the hot tears coming, I take a few deep breaths. I gather myself and my scripted, bony, uninspired lecture. I approach the lectern, leaning my bare, sweaty arm onto the coolness of the wood. My brain is not up to such a task as public speaking. Not yet. Maybe never again.

A cool draft shivers across my hot skin. I am cold. I am hot. I am ridiculous. These historical birthday guests are ridiculous. Mary Lincoln in her busy bonnet full of berries, now seated in a chair next to the lectern where I will soon be speaking, is ridiculous. The thought of me forming sentences is absolutely fucking ridiculous.

Mrs. Lincoln has been dead since 1882. Why does she need a birthday cake? Mack has been gone just two months. What can I ever say that will matter to me, to these people, to anyone? It is 132 years too late for Mary Lincoln, and it is a million years too soon for me. I do not care about my book. I do not give a whit for Mary Lincoln, although I am more sorry now than ever before for the mother's grief she suffered.

I want Mary Lincoln and all of these ridiculous people waiting to hear me speak to go away, to go poof into the air and leave me be. Squeezing my eyes shut, I beg for transport away from this damned room. Uber. Magic carpet. Whatever. I just need a vehicle big enough for me, my sorrows, and Mary's entire birthday cake. For all of my suffering, I deserve more than just one heavily frosted corner: I deserve to consume the cake alone and far, far away from here.

All of a sudden, at the back of the room, there is an excited murmur of voices. I look up, and the necks of the birthday guests are all craning towards the door. A tall, lanky figure dressed in a black suit with a loosened, crooked tie enters. He doffs his stovepipe hat to the room.

"Well, of course Mr. Lincoln is here," I say out loud.

How stupid I am for not having noticed his absence previously. This is his wife's birthday, for crying out loud, and this is Springfield, where Lincoln never died. This is the town in which he walks the streets at midnight and regularly shows up in unlikely places like nondescript conference rooms with molded plastic chairs. I laugh out loud, surprised at myself, and then stifle my laughter. I roll my eyes, because the ridiculous has just gotten even more ridiculous. As the people settle back into their seats and Mr. Lincoln finds one of his own, I laugh again. This time I let the rhythm of the laugh giggle through my muscles. I welcome the gentle relaxing of the tension in my jammed-up shoulders and my broken heart. The presence of Mr. Lincoln and my laughter have calmed my nerves.

I am not laughing because it is ridiculous that Abraham and Mary Lincoln are here and that we all accept them as being here. I mean, yes, that is ridiculous, but it is also ridiculous because this is not the first, or the second, or the third, fourth, or fifth time that I have delivered a lecture with Mr. Lincoln sitting in the audience. I laugh because for the last twenty years, this is what life has been for me as a Lincoln scholar living on Lincoln Avenue in Lincoln's hometown, where the spirit of the man is so much more than a ghost from the past.

It is all ridiculous, yes, but it is delightfully and brilliantly so, and through the fog of my grief and across my worries over the capacity of my brain to be coherent, I suddenly see my daughter's face. Mack is present, right here before my weary eyes. She is standing between me and Mrs. Lincoln, and she is laughing at me and at the happy absurdity of my life as a Lincoln scholar. She is scoffing, a mischievous grin perched like an imp below her freckled nose. She speaks to me, and I hear her say what she has said to me a hundred times before: "Lincoln is dead, Mom. You know that, right?"

"Not tonight he isn't," I say. "And neither are you, my sweet girl. Mr. Lincoln is right over there, and you're here." I tap two fingers over my heart. "I'm here, too," I whisper, almost believing it.

This is me out in the world. At this moment, I am not hidden away in my darkened bedroom where my despair has no witness. I am alive. I am miserable, but I am breathing, and I am not alone. Mack is here. Mr. and Mrs. Lincoln are here. And if I focus my eyes on the back of the room, where my dearest friends in all of the world have assembled to get me through this terrible first lecture after Mack, I might just get through this night. And when it's over, whatever happens, I'll reward myself with a giant piece of Mary's birthday cake.

I straighten my back and tell myself to draw power from all of the wonderful weirdness of this evening, to do this thing I do not want to do for all of these Lincoln-loving people in the room, if not for myself. Anyway, oh my God, there is absolutely nothing to get me out of it now, because the hostess is introducing me. She's calling me to take the podium. People are clapping, waiting for me to take my place. My inner voice is soft like the squeak of a tiny mouse, but my brain can hear it. I will do this for Mack. For cake. For me. I step up to the lectern and face the room.

G is for Gratitude

~

Daiva Markelis

November 4, 2016

I'm sitting in Zensaki, a restaurant in downtown Perth, Australia, watching little plates of sushi, sashimi, maki, and food that I can't identify pass me by on a conveyor belt that circles around the room. You grab the plates you desire. They all look delicious, but I'm afraid that in my eagerness, I'll reach for an ikra and dislodge the other plates from their moorings. There will be sushi all over the tables and the floor, and I'll be thrown out of Zensaki forever. So I order from the menu and realize how long it's been since I've used chopsticks. Or had sushi. Marty's not a sushi lover, and we live in Charleston, Illinois. Enough said.

There are sushi places everywhere. Five on this stretch of Barrack Street alone. There are Korean BBQs and dim sum cafés and Filipino eateries and Indian restaurants. Only one McDonalds, as far as I can tell. No Starbucks. My stereotype of Australia as a land of beefy rugby players is replaced by an image of a place with almost as many Asian Australians as husky white Aussies. What we term interracial couples back home are so common here that the term loses its meaning. At least in Perth. I have to be careful not to generalize. We go to Melbourne next, and maybe everyone will look Icelandic.

I pay for my bento and wander over to the Art Gallery of Western Australia. Museums are free, as are the city buses that take you to the museums. The gallery is housed in an unassuming building near several other museums. Inside—gleaming wooden floors, comfortable yet edgy black leather benches, huge rooms. Most of the paintings are huge as well: sweeping landscapes, oversized human bodies, large abstract canvasses by Aboriginal artists. There's a disturbing Lucian Freud, *Naked Man with Rat*, in the same room where some kind of performance art is taking place. At least I think it's performance art. There's a table with chairs in the middle of the room. Two women are talking very loudly about sex. There are three wigs on the table—blonde, red, and dark brown. In a corner of the room, there's a man sitting on a metal folding chair. Above him, a sign reads Sex Talk. I hurry out—I'm anxious I'll somehow be pulled into this unsettling tableau.

I get a coffee next door and then walk back to our hotel along the banks of the Swan River, once called the Black Swan River because of the black swans found here. When it comes to West Australian wildlife, I prefer the kookaburras because they're less pretentious, having no ambitions to be ballet dancers. I walk slowly. I am no ballet dancer. A few days ago, I tripped while walking down Adelaide Terrace. I landed on my hands and knees—the minimal dog pose in yoga, I think they call it. Several construction workers ran to my aid, helped me up, asked whether I needed an ambulance. Okay, maybe they didn't ask whether I needed an ambulance, but that's what I told Marty.

As I near the hotel, I realize it's been a long time since I've felt this happy, despite my scraped knees, despite my emotionally noncompliant husband (when he's playing in a Scrabble tournament). Perhaps it's the sun. The sun here is beautiful—better than the sun we have back home. It's better because November in Australia is spring verging on summer. November in Central Illinois is either winter or a strange lunatic summer (thanks, global warming) where birds are confused, and mutant green ladybugs converge upon doorsteps and windowsills.

And being near water makes me happy. Give me a lake or an ocean, and I will rush in like a fool, arms flapping, not bothering to check the temperature or consider the fact that I'm not a very good swimmer. Give me a swimming pool, and I will dog-paddle my way from one end to the other.

Yesterday, as Marty was playing Games 23 to 26 of the World Scrabble Tournament, I went whale watching.

"I saw whales," I bragged to Marty later. "Two or maybe three."

"If you're not sure of the number, they may have just been figments of your imagination."

"The company has a 98% percent success rate in sighting whales. Read the brochure."

"They probably send out big wooden planks into the ocean every morning. And then point them out as whales."

"I'm pretty sure what I saw were not wooden planks, unless they were wooden planks jumping out of the water."

I could have gone swimming with dolphins: wild dolphins, not those poor creatures in Florida that are kept in dolphinariums and have to endure tourists pawing over them and taking selfies. The brochures here stated you can't feed or touch the dolphins, just swim side by side with them. I was fearful I might get one of those (rightfully) resentful dolphins that are sick and tired of people swimming in their territory. Also, the price for the swim was $200. And the tour operators make you wear a wetsuit. I was afraid I wouldn't be able to get into the wetsuit or, worse, get out of the wetsuit. I'd have to waddle back to the hotel looking like a giant drunk penguin.

I didn't go swimming with dolphins. But I saw a whale.

And today I had sushi.

And there was sun.

Goddess

~

Marty Gabriel

"Daiva … means "goddess," she told me.
"It's a lot to live up to."

You have to like a goddess
who can laugh at herself … and you …
though not as much as she might …
especially at you, an angel
with so much to learn about life,
art, and poems that don't rhyme.

She beguiles and bewitches,
languorous, bearish, and good.
Constant, yet capricious, too,
more playful than pouty, thank … God?

Her time is precious
and so are her patience, trust, and love.

Her loving grows with tenderness,
properly guarded: it grows
to elicit wonder and spasms of joy
befitting an earthly goddess, I hope.

Mixed Signals

~

Charlotte England

"Warm ... leatherette ... warm .... leatherette ..."

I was mystified. The words made no sense. The monotonous backbeat and low, vaguely threatening vocals would have given me the creeps if they hadn't been so patently absurd. Perhaps there was irony at work here? I wouldn't put it past him! At the point where the warm leatherette melted onto burning flesh, I hit fast forward and landed in the next track, an up-tempo number reminiscent of the Beatles. This was better. Slightly giddy voices sang about the joy induced by an equestrian statue "prancing up and down the square."

I couldn't remember King Edward VII ever making me feel that way when I crossed Queen's Park, but the thundering harpsichord was fun. The song got a bit manic towards the end, but I couldn't help smiling. Who was this strange boy?

Yesterday he arrived at my dorm room in the middle of my Latin homework and parked himself in the armchair in front of the window. I made tea, glad of an interruption, since the sentences for translation were horribly dull. Mugs and biscuit tin produced, we chatted for a few minutes, and then he said, "Can I read you a poem?"

Since the most recent of our spring misunderstandings had been cleared up, I'd heard quite a few of Richard's poems. They were strange but rather good: thoughtful, evocative, and worth talking over. I said I'd love to hear the latest, so he pulled out some lecture notes, in the margins of which he had scrawled a short verse.

"It's called 'Dearest K,' and I think it's a letter written by a soldier in wartime to a sweetheart back home."

The little lyric was surprisingly tender.

"Wow. I like it. But how odd. Not like anything you've read me before."

"Usually I write on the subway. It helps me forget I'm stuck in an enclosed space speeding through darkness. I'm a little claustrophobic. Writing helps me not get out before I reach downtown. But this isn't a subway poem."

The late afternoon sun streamed in behind him, touching the coppery lights in his hair and casting his face into shadow. He was earnest today, no trace of the faintly mocking "antic disposition" he sometimes adopted. This was the Richard I preferred and got glimpses of from time to time when he dropped in for tea.

"When did you write this?"

"In zoology."

"During class?" I tried not to sound scandalized: the penny loafers, knitted tie, and Latin homework were bad enough.

"It was dull, and I couldn't concentrate. I've got things on my mind."

"What sort of things?"

"The poem, for one. Suddenly it came into my head, and I forgot all about LRS."

"LRS?"

"An organism's life reproductive success—the prof was droning on about it."

"Why a soldier?"

"I don't know."

"And who's K?"

He looked at me very thoughtfully and hesitated a moment before replying.

"I think it's you."

"Me?"

"Mmmhmmm."

"But it's a love poem."

"Yes."

My mind reeled. Richard and I had been getting along much better, but he was officially Margaret's boyfriend. I felt distinctly out of my depth and said something inadequate to gain time.

"You're an odd fish!"

"Can I swim in your aquarium?"

After that, we took a long walk north of campus towards Casa Loma, block after block of earnest, confusing, surprising conversation. That was yesterday. This afternoon, still torn between delight and bewilderment but having gone to class anyway, I returned to my room to find a mixtape titled "Dearest K" on my transom. Richard used to carry these sometimes, along with other oddities—including, once, parts of a telephone—in his pockets. They served as "conversation starters" when he visited friends at St. Hilda's, but this one, it seemed, was just for me. A note stated that he had chosen the things on it to introduce himself, as it were, musically.

On the spot, I decided to retaliate in kind, but not until I had heard all of it. After "Warm Leatherette" and "The Equestrian Statue," things improved for a bit with some folksongs by Steeleye Span. In one of them a maid "as white as any milk" refuses the advances of a black smith she describes as "husky, dusky, fusky, (and) musky" by changing herself into a series of different forms. He, ever resourceful, transforms himself too. She becomes a rose and he a bumblebee; she takes the veil, and he becomes a priest; when she opts to be a corpse, he turns into the clay of her grave.

Well, that was endearing. Oh no, the Bonzo Dog Band again —in lounge lizard noir mode—back to the slightly threatening Richard. Johnny Cool describes his encounter with a dame called Hotsie whose chief distinguishing features appeared to be numerical "48-23-38."

In the end, though, my heart was won by Billy Bragg, an unlikely outcome for a strait-laced miss who preferred French chansons and Bach to wailing socialist folksingers, but who could resist the offer of an "extra pint" from the "milkman of human kindness".

Lines Writ While Lot Was Going to the Pop Machine in the Basement

~

Richard England

Lost Kings, long-dead Emperors and Jarls
Prophet-Lords ten thousand years since dust,
The Wheel of Ages, turning, has crushed
your mighty lands, your reigns and hegemonies
into shards of prehistoric memories—
the occasional matter to divert
a century of distracted, scholarly, irresolute minds.
It is good that you are dust,
not that I cry out against your kind,
mad despots, great leaders, cunning autocrats,
strong generals wielding an army as if it were
a well-balanced knife, inspired theocrats
blazing with light and igniting the nations
like lightning fallen on dry woods.
Lost kings, you are lucky to be lost!
For if you knew now what you lacked
when all the world was yours, you would wish
yourselves to oblivion in your jealousy.
For none of you ever had,
for all your golden ages and your glory—
a Queen like mine.

A Patriotic Family
~
Roxanne Frey

A WWII navy brat became an army wife during Vietnam. Added the title of Military Mom when her son was sent to Iraq. Her granddaughter put on an air force uniform, so now she is a Wing Grandma. When the music starts, she stands tall, hand over her heart, brown eyes wet.

Listen to Me

~

Johnni Olds

Travis wouldn't shut up about the love of his life walking out on him. Although drinking wasn't involved, he burst into song about drowning his sorrow in whiskey.

After two hours of this, he thanked people for listening to him, then walked off the Nashville concert stage into the open arms of his loving wife.

Painting with Words

~

Janet Messenger

A sheet of paper lies before me, a blank canvas awaiting my thoughts. Within my head lies the idea, the story, and a yearning to write what I'm feeling and experiencing. As a dreamer, I imagine the place, the characters, the situation, the emotion, the dialogue. As a writer, I paint the scenarios with words.

White Paper

~

Madeline Ignazito

I stare at the blank white screen
And the pulsing cursor—
That bane of my existence,
Staring back
Winking, blinking
Over and over again!

Does it ever stop?

Of course, turning the computer off
Would stop it, but the problem would still be there.

My old teacher used to say
Dance around the waste basket!

In today's world, the waste basket is the delete button,
One does not dance but solemnly pushes a key.

What to write or what not to write?

Any words will do for now
Just keep typing to keep ahead
Of that blinking #@&* cursor.

Curse the cursor!

There, I said it.
Maybe now I can settle down.

The Greek House

~

Phyllis Bayles

Every home has its own smell: sometimes it's furniture polish, sometimes it's cooking spices, sometimes it's from pets. There's the "woodsy" smell from wooden beams or trim. The musty smell from the old couch brings back the days when you lay there and watched a tabletop TV. No matter where the smell comes from, every time you walk into that house, you know where you are. You are in familiar territory and your emotions react accordingly.

And in my senior years, there is one house with smells I still remember vividly.

In my home town of Danville, Illinois, the immigrants from Greece formed a community of several families. Many of the women were brides who came through Ellis Island. They came to join the men who had arrived several years earlier. These men had started businesses and were now ready to start families.

As the entire group became friends and shared their daily lives, they realized that it was time to establish a place that was theirs alone. It needed to be a place where they could gather to practice their customs, preserve their language, and hold fast to the music and foods of their homeland. Greek school was very important, and they needed rooms, tables, and chairs for classes, but most of all, they needed a place in which to worship according to their Greek Orthodox religion.

The men started looking for that place. One day, a sign went up in front of a big two-story white house. It was set on a small hill overlooking Seminary Street. My dad convinced the other men to go and take a look. He asked them to use their imaginations. It had large rooms, perfect for conversion to a chapel. There was a big kitchen. Could they see the lambs roasting and the *pastitsio* baking in the giant oven? They looked at the pantries, which would hold plates, cups, saucers, and silverware for their parties and gatherings. One of the bedrooms could house the visiting priests who would come to hold services. Across the street was a school with a playground where the children could go to play, and, best of all, the entire upstairs could be turned into an apartment. The rental would pay the mortgage.

SOLD! The Greek House was established.

The house on Seminary Street in Danville, Illinois became the center of the Greek immigrant community. Eventually it was consecrated as St. Barbara Chapel and became sacred ground. If you were going for church services, when you climbed up the front steps and reached the porch, the smell of burning candles and incense enveloped you. You lit your candle. You pressed two fingers and your thumb together very tightly "so the devil can't get through." Then you made the sign of the cross, from your right side to the left, ending over your heart. Maybe you were there for the Divine Liturgy or for a wedding. Maybe you were there for a baptism or for the beautiful Easter services. But always, when you walked in, the Greek House smelled of incense and candles.

Was it a birthday party? A graduation party? An engagement party? When you opened the front door, the Greek House smelled like something delicious was being cooked in that big kitchen. The rooms were fragrant with a mixture of oregano, onions, cheeses, olives, baked chickens or lamb, and made-from-scratch tomato sauce.

My favorite smells came in December. The ladies would gather to begin making pastries for their annual bake sale. If you've ever smelled fresh baklava, made with cinnamon and nuts and dripping in honey, then you know what it is to have your mouth water. And the Greeks, as the saying goes, had a word for it: "I salivated." The common expression (always said with gusto) was "Peh sah neh ta salia mou!"

When the men decided to spruce up the house, or even renovate, you were enveloped by smells of paint, lumber, new carpeting. There was even the undertone of sweaty armpits.

At other times, and on special occasions, you smelled the mixture of the various perfumes the ladies wore. I don't recall anyone complaining of allergies, but maybe that explained why certain people always sat near the windows.

Over sixty-five years later, the house is still there. Today, the Greek community is very small. Yet those still there keep the place in good shape. It's still used for all the same reasons. When I go back to visit and enter the Greek House, I know I'm in the place that was where all our days were filled with true friends, close family, and precious memories.

Isn't it amazing how the simple smells of one house can bring so many memories of transformative experiences flooding back?

Pantespani (Παντεσπάνι)

*Want to experience the scent of spices and citrus? Try this recipe.
The use of orange or lemon and cinnamon give it a lovely taste and
fabulous aroma.*

*Pantespani is a traditional light sponge cake, soaked in a light syrup. It
can be served as is, with toppings such as whipped cream and
strawberries (similar to strawberry shortcake), with some toasted
almonds, or other toppings of your choice, and without the syrup as any
other sponge cake.*

Make the syrup first:
1 cup sugar
3/4 cup water
1 cinnamon stick
Juice of 1 orange or one lemon, pick your favorite
*Combine all ingredients and gently boil for about 15 minutes, or until
candy thermometer reaches 205 degrees. Hint—toss one of the 1/2
rinds right in there with it.*
Set aside

*Make the cake: But first grease and flour a 13 by 9 inch pan. Set oven to
350*
*5 eggs separated——the yellows to a mixing bowl, the whites to a smaller
mixing bowl*
1 cup sugar
1 cup cake flour
1 1/4 tsp baking powder
Pinch of salt
1 lemon or orange rind, grated
1 tsp vanilla
1/2 cup melted butter

*Beat egg yolks and sugar until light and creamy.
Sift dry ingredients together and gradually add to batter. Mix in citrus
rind and vanilla.
Beat egg whites until stiff. Fold gently into batter*

Pour into the pan.

Spoon melted butter over the top.
Bake at 350 for 25-30 minutes
Remove from oven and gently spoon syrup all over the top.
Let it set for a while before serving. Cake can be made the day ahead.
If you make with lemon, blueberries are a delicious topping.
If you make with orange, top with strawberries or peaches.

Sulfur, Sassafras, and Dandelions

~

Hannah Eads

When I was a child, at the first sign of springtime, my mother would open all of the windows to let in the crisp, fresh spring air. "This rids the house of all of the stuffy winter air," she would say. Then she placed a small yellow cake of sulfur on the big old black iron cookstove. I remember the strong odor coming from the billowing cloud of sulfur. "It purifies the air," Mom remarked.

Another springtime tradition that I recall is the brewing of sassafras tea. Mom would drop chunks of red sassafras bark into the teapot that was kept simmering on the stove. I enjoyed smelling the aroma of that lovely pink tea, which had a delicate, sweet taste; drinking a cup of tea with my mother made me feel grown up.

And every spring, Mom gathered the young green dandelion leaves that she then rinsed and boiled in a big pot. She would serve these greens with a dash of vinegar at the dinner table and encourage us to try some. "It will purify your blood," she told us. I don't know if that was true, but I never ate any because I didn't like the bitter taste.

Spring cleaning meant taking all of the rugs out of the house and throwing them over the clothesline in the backyard. I liked to help beat out the dust using an old wire rug beater. "It will give you strong muscles," she told me. Mom had learned all these rituals from her mother, and it seemed that she wanted to carry on the family traditions.

However, there is one family tradition that Mom didn't continue. Every spring, my grandmother Hannah would make dandelion wine. Neither my mother nor my father ever drank, so Mom never made the wine. She saved the recipe, and I shared it with a friend, who made a batch and gave me a bottle. It is light and sweet.

Dandelion Wine

1 gallon boiling water
1 quart dandelion blossoms and stems
3 oranges, unpeeled and sliced
3 lemons, unpeeled and sliced
3 pounds sugar
one-half yeast cake

Pour boiling water over dandelions, orange slices, and lemon slices. Allow to stand three days, then strain. Add sugar and yeast. Let stand four or five days. Bottle and cork loosely until fermentation has stopped. Then cork tightly and store in a cool, dark place.

Alexander's

~

Jane Gilbert

Back before Eastern Illinois State Teachers College became EIU, back before Lincoln Avenue became Highway 16, back before Walmart, the courthouse square was the commercial hub of Charleston. All the storefronts were filled with local businesses, and everyone in town came there to shop for whatever they needed. There were three thriving drugstores, three shoe stores, a couple of jewelry shops, several little restaurants, and much more. Benedict's Five and Dime anchored the north side, along with the Dress Well, an upscale women's apparel store. Today we'd call it a boutique, but in the 1940s, we'd never heard that word. The south side held Frommel's hardware, where my father shopped while my mother was buying groceries at the A&P just a few doors away. Penney's was on the west side, and on the east side of the square, at the corner of Jackson, was Alexander's Department Store, Charleston's answer to Marshall Field's.

Alexander's did their best to create at least the illusion of the big-city shopping experience. The first thing you saw were the display windows, three storefronts wide, decorated in seasonal themes, with mannequins dressed in the latest fashions. As you walked in the front door, there were the sparkling glass cases of jewelry and cosmetics and the heady aromas of the perfume department. If you wandered in further, you came to handbags, accessories, sweaters, blouses, and intimate apparel.

At the back of the store, a wide staircase led up to a mezzanine balcony with no merchandise, only desks and clicking machinery. Further stairs led to a second floor with dresses, coats, and a shoe department, where you sat in a comfortable chair while a patient clerk measured your feet and then brought out endless boxes of shoes in your size for you to try.

There was also a basement level, definitely a no-frills place with harsher lighting, narrower aisles, and much less attractive displays. Here, you could find a toy department, a few housewares, and all the bargain-rate merchandise.

My clothes didn't come from Alexander's; they came from Penney's across the square. But my mother sometimes shopped there for herself and for gifts at Christmastime, and I usually accompanied her. I enjoyed going to Alexander's with her because the store was attractive, and I liked looking at all the treasures it held and because everyone who worked there was nice to you. But there were two things about that store that were unique in Charleston and therefore of special interest to a curious child. One was their method of handling money.

All transactions were in cash. When you made a purchase at any counter in the store, the clerk would write up the sale on a pad of slips with a carbon duplicate listing the item, purchase price, and sales tax. Then she took your money, and both slips of paper and put them into a little cylinder about the size of a soup can that attached to a line over her head. She pulled on a handle, and the cylinder shot along that line and up to a faceless cashier on the mezzanine. A minute or so later, the cylinder would return with your change and the duplicate sales slip. I had seen a similar system in large Chicago stores, but this was the only one of its kind in Charleston. It was great fun to walk through the store, hear the whoosh, and see those little vehicles zipping up to their mysterious destination. I found it fascinating but also puzzling. I never could understand what made the cylinder go.

The other attraction for a child of six or seven was the elevator with an operator whose only job was to take you from the ground floor to the second floor or to the basement and then to bring you back again with all those purchases you were sure to make. I only ever saw one person in that job. She might have suffered from dwarfism—she had a seriously deformed back—but was always well-groomed, neatly dressed, and friendly in a properly respectful way. I especially liked her because she was my size, and I could look her in the eye. The elevator looked like a cage with a door that folded in on itself. It was quite small, with just enough room for the operator and perhaps three or four passengers. It operated with a lever on a wheel that the lady moved from vertical to nine-o'clock or three o'clock to make the car go up or down. I was fascinated by all of it. I loved to ride the elevator, and my earliest life's ambition was to be an elevator operator when I grew up. As far as I knew, it was the only elevator in town—at least the only one for use by the public.

Sometime in the fifties, Alexander's suffered a major fire. By then, the geography of commerce in Charleston had started to change. Eastern was growing and becoming more economically significant. The Illinois Department of Highways moved Route 16 from Madison to Lincoln Avenue, and then Walmart came to town. Alexander's was sold by its local owner to a minor chain, the name was changed, and finally, the store closed for good. The space became a facility for services to the handicapped and today stands empty like many of its neighbors. I don't go up to the square very often any more, but when I do, I have fond memories of Alexander's.

Foreign Invasion of an Unknown Kind

~

Madeline Ignazito

There is a shadow there
Within me—what it is will be to come …
What it will be, is to be.
There is a shadow of a nodule—
A breath of darkness—oppressing my mind
With the Ray of the unknown (x)
X unknown—unwanted
Be nigh Be nigh.

Again, I wait, as many times before, the waiting unendurable. The mind goes in circles like ripples in water disturbed by a thrown rock…

It is like floating suspended—a little droplet held in an opaque glass—fully immersed and drowning in the murky, spongy, grayish liquid, shaking and quivering.

It is a terrifying time to learn if one is to die or not. It will take all my strength and intelligence to live through this. However, there are beacons of light from those I love. For them I must be brave. I must be strong and courageous. I must be Okay.

Being in limbo in the world of the unknown, waiting for results of biopsies and mammograms, is more frightening than the reality, one way or the other. There are so many strange thoughts floating in my brain.

My appointment with the white-robed man of medicine is here. At last a result, but instead I am told they want more views, as again they see calcifications, but they probably are benign. Again, the hurtful squishing exam (no doubt invented by a man). Of course they decided to have five different views. More compression of my body to shapes that it was not meant to be. Everyone is kind and thoughtful. They know what I am going through. Many before me and many yet to come have trodden and will tread the same path. I am told that the results will be given to me tomorrow. I keep myself busy and read myself to sleep.

Surprisingly, I sleep well. I wake early and go and get our mail. I tell my husband that the worst scenario would be a mastectomy. My mind redirects itself, thinking hopefully that probably it is okay, since we have not heard yet. To Greenup I go, to my massage appointment. What a relief that is, forgetting to leave my cell phone on. When I come home, there is a little note on the table from my husband saying that everything is *okay*! They will see me next year to repeat the same fiasco again. I have now reached the fifth year of survival cancer-free. I am joyful and so very grateful.

Final Visit

~

June Hayden

In memory of my father, who passed away May 2, 1994

I stare out the window of the quiet room where I sit with my family. It is a lovely spring day, the first day of May, and I watch through the glass as the birds flit happily from one shrub to another. Outside, the world is bursting forth with life, but death looms heavily within these walls. I glance at the old man on the bed, with his gaunt face and scrawny arms.

"That is not my dad," I silently scream. My thoughts turn to the father I have known for most of my life....

Dad worked in a factory and was a backyard mechanic on weekends. I remember his muscled arms and sinewy hands, always black from grease and oil, and smile to myself. *I don't think I ever saw Dad with clean hands until he came to live in the nursing home*, I muse. Dad's favorite place was his garage, where he spent most of his spare time. It was like his retreat, a place he could go to escape the responsibilities of providing for a family of five and do the kind of work he enjoyed so much.

The garage was large. Dad had built it himself, and he wanted to have plenty of room. Having a self-expressed hatred of "dungeons," he had left the entire south side of the building open, and on sunny days, my siblings and I liked to hang out on the concrete pad that extended the width of the southern opening.

Dad almost always had a radio playing, and we enjoyed listening with him to country music, to various radio ministers, and especially to the Indianapolis 500 race, which took place every Memorial Day. Often, his radio blaring in the background, we would see Dad working at the bench grinder he had mounted on a large wooden post set in the ground just outside the garage.

Since he had known nothing but hard manual labor all his life, Dad's only hobby was work. So, in order to keep busy after retiring from his factory job, he became caretaker for several local cemeteries. And the month of May became one of the busiest times of the year for him. After a long winter's hibernation, the young blades of grass pushed enthusiastically through the warm soil, eagerly soaking up the rays of sunshine and gentle spring rains.

The little wisps grew rapidly, soon carpeting the cemetery grounds with a plush green cover. Arriving toward the month's end, Memorial Day always brought a host of visitors who came to decorate graves of loved ones. And of course, these annual pilgrims expected the grounds to be well manicured. So, early in the month, Dad would stand at the bench grinder and sharpen his mower blades, preparing them for the grass-cutting season ahead.

Back in Dad's room, I am only vaguely aware of the television, which is playing in the background, for my attention remains focused on the bed where my father lies, his life slowly ebbing away as we all sit in silence, listening to the shallow breaths grow weaker and farther apart and wondering which one might be the last. Suddenly the melancholy of the moment is interrupted by the sound of engines revving as the sportscaster announces the latest reports from the racing time trials in Indianapolis. I had almost forgotten about the Indianapolis 500 auto race coming up at month's end, and I smile at the memory of listening to the race with Dad many years ago and at the realization that if he were still able to work, Dad would no doubt be at his bench grinder sharpening mower blades right now.

The next morning, we received the message we knew was inevitable—Dad had passed away at 1:00 a.m. We spent the rest of the day taking care of the usual necessary tasks—calling other family members, making arrangements for the services, finding something to wear, etc. By evening, we were worn out, and we slept soundly that night, no longer concerned that our slumber would be interrupted by "the call" we had so dreaded to receive.

Tuesday morning, Mom phoned to say she had just received a call from their neighbors in the country. Although they had moved to town several years ago, Mom and Dad were unwilling to sell the ten-acre country plot where our childhood home and Dad's beloved garage still stood—there were just too many memories. The neighbors had become self-appointed guardians of the property, quickly reporting to my parents any unusual sights, sounds, or activities they observed. This was the reason for the phone call that morning. After the usual condolences, the neighbors reported they had heard a noise the night before and thought perhaps someone should come and check it out.

My husband was conscripted to perform the investigation. After arriving at the property, he parked his vehicle and began to look around. He saw no one and, for that matter, found no evidence of any recent visitors. However, he did hear a noise that sounded like a piece of machinery running, and it appeared to be emanating from the vicinity of Dad's garage. He continued following the sound until he discovered the source—it was the bench grinder! The grinder had not been turned on since Dad had last used it about three years ago, but it was running now.

Chills raced up and down my spine as Jim related the story to me. Who would have turned on the grinder, and why? Neither of us was able to conjure any sort of feasible scenario to answer that question. Was the whole incident just some kind of strange coincidence? Or....

My heart beat rapidly as I considered the possibility that Dad had asked St. Peter to take a detour on their journey to the pearly gates. Perhaps this episode with the bench grinder had been Dad's way of saying goodbye and letting us know he had stopped by for one final visit.

Warm

~

Jane Gilbert

When she curls up at the end of the bed, she warms my feet. When she nuzzles my face in the morning to wake me up, she warms my cheek. But when she climbs onto my lap, lays her head in the crook of my elbow, and purrs herself to sleep, she warms my heart.

The Touch

~

June Hayden

We gaze into each other's eyes. Oblivious to my surroundings, I inch closer, my attention focused only on those eyes. And then it happens—the electrifying touch! I shriek, though not with delight, and recoil from the fence. She continues to stare as her calves finish their supper, unaware of either me or my camera.

Oops
~
Janet Messenger

I struck up a conversation with Mary
and heard her say,
"I recently got a divorce."
I was shocked, speechless.
Happily, she continued…
"He's not here now but will be soon,
I already have a stall for him."
Suddenly I realized
she had said, "I got a new horse!"
Time to get my hearing checked.

The Stoner Drive Canine Patrol Unit

~

Janet Messenger

Hear that? That's one of my buddies on street patrol, a member of our neighborhood canine patrol, woofing it up. If I read his bark correctly, something suspicious raised his hackles and he's broadcasting an APB (all-points bulletin) to the other members of the Stoner Canine Patrol Unit—Patrol Unit for short, or shorter yet...the PUs.

We work undercover—no uniforms. Our only IDs are the rabies tags on our collars. We're on duty 24/7 guarding the neighborhood against burglars, kidnappers, salesmen, delivery persons, deer, squirrel, raccoons, or other varmints foolish enough to enter our territory.

Five of us make up the unit—Silly, Dizzy, Bo, Riley, and me, Milo. Each has a special talent that contributes to our ability to solve crimes and keep the neighborhood safe.

Silly, a black lab, possesses supersonic hearing and a loud bark that can frighten any PERP (perpetrator) who dares set foot in the neighborhood. She follows commands well and holds a graduation certificate from Obedience School. She's now taking additional training from our FTO (field training officer), Gina.

Dizzy, a big bruiser of a chocolate lab, is the reconnaissance officer. He patrols the perimeter, sniffing out and marking all trees, low lying bushes, and garbage cans, searching for MUTTS (extremely unsavory characters) who may be lurking in the shadows.

Riley, a German Shepherd mix, tends to stray outside the neighborhood perimeter. Several times we've had to issue an APB for her, so she's been assigned Special Squirrel Duty in her own yard. She's solely responsible for quelling riots involving juvenile squirrel gangs and robberies involving walnuts.

Bo, a handsome chocolate lab, is the youngest squad member, a JUVIE (juvenile). He has a lot of potential and has been trained for field work and hunting. Bo located several DBs (dead bodies) and rolled on them to collect DNA samples for identification purposes. He usually works alone.

As senior squad member, I'm referred to as Chief Milo. Most days my shift is spent at headquarters mapping out strategies and tactics for the squad. I'm researching and writing a training manual for the SCPU based on case-solving tactics aired on two TV dramas—*Blue Bloods* and *Miami Vice*—along with some *Dirty Harry* movies.

Sorry. Got to go. Just heard a UTL (unable to locate) code coming from the kitchen, and it's about meal time. 10-20, good buddy.

"Dear Milo" Advice Columnist

~

Janet Messenger

Hi. Milo here.

With Valentine's Day right around the corner, I've been thinking a lot about love and life lately. I know a lot about life because I'm living it, plus I pay close attention to the wise advice Dr. Phil gives on TV. Janet keeps me abreast of local and national events by reading aloud articles from newspapers and magazines, and I also keep tabs on happenings in the neighborhood. All that, combined with a good dose of canine common sense, is all I need to write an advice column. Right?

My column would be similar to Dear Abby, but different because my solutions to life's ups and downs would come from a dog's point of view, not biased or influenced by human complexities. Dogs don't rely on fancy theories or big words: we tell it like it is. You know that dogs are loyal creatures: honest, caring, faithful, and true. They display the same qualities as Boy Scouts. They know how to survive in the world, and they mature at a faster pace than humans do: one year of human life is equal to seven years of mine. Dogs also have role models—Lassie and Rin Tin Tin—two of the smartest canines to ever walk the planet.

To prove I'd make a good advice columnist, give me a hypothetical situation, and I'll give you my best advice.

Hypothetical Situation: A lovestruck young man in a dither wants to impress his dream girl.

Dear Milo:

My love life is on the skids. My hours just got cut at McDonald's, and Valentine's Day is only a couple weeks away. I have a crush on this real "hot" chick and want to impress her. She comes in every day during my shift and orders a Big Mac, fries, a diet coke, and a hot fudge sundae from the $1 menu. I know she likes me, 'cause I'm the one who always takes her order. She smiles and winks at me. A couple times, she even held my hand for what seemed like an eternity when I gave her back the change.

Milo, here's my problem. I may not be here when she comes in next time since my work schedule is changing. How do I let her know I think she's real special and I'd like to take her to a cheap— I mean, movie that fits my budget?

Signed, $1 Menu Dilemma

My Answer:

Dear $1 Menu Dilemma:

Next time "Hot Chick" comes in and you take her order, tell her your work schedule is changing and you'd be really sorry if you missed talking to her, since she's your favorite customer. When you give her back her change, reach into your pocket and slip in a little handwritten note saying "Happy Valentine's Day! Like to catch a movie some time? My treat!" Sign it "Dilemma" (but use your real name).

Draw a couple hearts on the note and put your phone number on it. Ask her what kind of movies she likes. Whatever her answer is, say that's your favorite too. Tell her you'd love to take her to an early movie and ask her to give you a jingle (FYI, early shows have the cheapest ticket prices). Smile real nice and be sure you've brushed your teeth and used a good mouthwash, so your breath is minty fresh. You're bound to make an impression. Good luck.

Milo

Well, how did I do? Think Dear Abby will worry about the competition?

Mary Had a Little Lamb

~

Johnni Olds

When Daddy was a dairy farmer in Kentucky, we had all kinds of animals, but one was almost like a member of the family. It was a cute little lamb whose mother had disowned her and her brother. Daddy named them Lula Belle and Scotty after a couple of country singers.

Lula Belle is a good name for a lamb, don't you think? She and my sister, Mary, took a liking to each other. Mary so loved the lambs that my parents let them live in the house during the winter. Daddy built a pen and placed it by the stove. My sister babied Lula Belle by feeding her with a bottle. Now that I think of it, I guess it was a family affair to spoil that lamb. She really had it "made in the shade"!

As they grew, they both went back to the herd, but Lula Belle was unhappy. She always ran down the long, winding driveway to greet Mary and my brother, Eddie, when they got off the school bus. I guess she thought she was a little girl and Mary and Eddie were her parents. Scotty decided he was a sheep and stayed with the herd, but Lula Belle was perfectly happy as a little girl.

Mary was followed by Lula Belle everywhere she went, even the bathroom. She went to bed with Mary, slept at the bottom of the bed, and woke up when Mary did. Lula Belle did everything my sister did, so on the first day of school, she somehow crossed the cattle guard and marched right onto the school bus! This was very much to the delight of the children, and they started singing a song that fit the occasion perfectly. You can probably guess what it was. Of course, we all know it was against the rules to take a lamb to school, so it was a sad day for both Mary and Lula Belle when the bus driver carried the lamb off the bus while she was crying *baa-baa-baa.*

Frankensheep

~

Charlotte England

I suppose there are stranger ways to redeem the time than spending a Sunday morning doing dog toy taxidermy, but my current project is pretty bizarre. The sorry brown specimen on my sewing table was once a well-loved beaver. Now, deprived of tail and voice, it has been cast aside by the poodles in favor of more vital and intact stuffies. Conscious that what I am doing might constitute an act of imaginative trespass worthy of Dr. Moreau, I begin cutting apart "Beavertje" in order to make a good-sized pelt with which to repair Ding-a-ling, the Sheep of Death.

For seven and a half years, Ding-y has been Pippa's refuge in times of uncertainty. As a pup, she picked out this sheep from a pile of toys at an outdoor flea market, apparently entranced by the jingling copper bell around its neck. From that day to this, it has remained her most treasured possession, but time has not been kind to Ding-a-ling. Early on, the sheep got washed occasionally, but Ding is large and takes the better part of three hot, sunny days to dry, during which Pip's anxiety level soars, so the white, wooly exterior has been allowed to get very grubby. Pip's more or less daily habit of chewing Ding-y to soothe herself has also compromised the toy's structural integrity to the point where washing is no longer possible. Ding-a-ling stinks, but Pip remains loyal. Numerous attempts to replace it with cleaner toys have proven fruitless. Eventually Richard and I just shrugged our shoulders and decided to take our chances living in close proximity to the Plague Sheep. When guests arrive and Pip carries the grimy, beloved toy to the door, we apologize and wonder if they will ever visit again.

Enter Ciaran. At almost five months old, he has been with us for just half his short life, and despite our best efforts, he does not yet know how to respect taboos. Ciri was ten pounds when he arrived, and while the nickname Squidgy still suited him, Ding-a-ling was safe. Now, however, Cir is three-quarters Pippa's size, and the game has changed. Early this morning, frustrated and grouchy after a bad night with a sinus infection, I headed for the tea kettle. In the hallway was a terrible scene: masses of fluffy white innards littered the floor from the bedroom to the front door. In the living room, lying on the carpet with a disconsolate Pip standing sadly over it, was a miserably deflated Ding-y. Cir the Disemboweler danced around the two of them, wholly insensitive to the psychic distress he had caused. For a moment I thought that we might, at last, be rid of public health hazard number one, but Pippa's distraught expression set me straight. I gathered up Dingy's insides, stuffed them where her tummy had been, and started thinking about restoration.

Attaching purple seam binding to the edges of some fake brown beaver fur makes my small sewing machine rebel. It is not alone. I have no clear idea of how I am going to do this. Sewing always takes longer than I think it will and requires a kind of visual imagination just beyond the edge of my skill set. Besides, my burgeoning to-do list has become a massive should-have-done-by-now one, thanks to a series of tedious health problems. At least my shoulder is working again, five weeks after a bad sprain, though whether it will continue to do so if I spend two hours jabbing a massive upholstery needle through Ding-a-ling's matted hide is an open question. Surely the last thing I should be doing today is working on Frankensheep.

An insistent golden paw presses my left thigh. Pip is worried. Ding-a-ling is sitting up here on the table next to my Pfaff, just out of reach. Hampered by an innate instinct for obedience, something that will probably never trouble Ciaran, Pip can't just rear up on her hind legs and grab it. I look into her imploring brown eyes, whisper words of reassurance, and stab myself on a neglected pin. Pip inches her bottom closer to my chair and paws my lap again. Why is she so attached to this stinky, horrible toy? Can't we just throw it out? Surely she is too old to need it?

And then I see it. Behind the long-suffering dowager duchess expression that Pip has adopted since Ciaran arrived, there is a glimpse of the pup she once was. In my mind's eye, I see Salisbury's open-air flea market on a sunny Saturday in May. There is a higgledy-piggledy assemblage of no-longer-useful-to-me, potentially-useful-to-you junk spread across a downtown parking lot. My bouncing, golden baby girl charges into the center of some old children's toys and seizes a snow-white sheep with a bright copper bell around its neck. She won't let go. Laughing, we shell out two dollars for a toy more or less the same size as our new puppy. She carries it through the rest of the market, only setting it down for a moment when, with one proprietary foot placed firmly on its back, she gets the last bite of the hotdog that her brother George has been eating.

So many times these last few weeks, I have looked at Pip when Ciaran's youthful antics seemed to annoy her and asked, "Don't you remember when you were a pup, Pip?" Such a rollicking little princess she was in those days, like sunshine poured into a furry, apricot-colored coat, lighting up every room she entered. I loved her to pieces then, as I have ever since: her joy and her freshness lightened many years made heavy by other things. This summer, as George lay dying, Pip grew solemn with her new responsibilities. When he left us, she seemed to age overnight. I had hoped that Ciaran's introduction would renew her youthful spark, but of course, it is all more complicated than that. After all, Cir is not a patch to cover a hole in our hearts: he is an emerging talent erupting on stage in the middle of a small company of improvisational actors who have worked together for years. He is young yet, and better at performing acrobatics than responding to dialogue cues. We'll have to work around Ciri until he grows into his natural role.

How do I apply this bit of purple-edged beaver pelt to the underside of Pip's sheep? I find myself saying a prayer for guidance, and a voice in my head runs a little interference. *Surely it is absurd to be praying about how to fix a disgusting toy! What sort of a God could you ask such a question of anyway?* But my heart insists that the problem is important as well as absurd. What kind of a God? One who asks us to stretch our hearts through acts of love that bring us out of ourselves and closer to Him.

Of course, the skeptical voice doesn't concede any ground: *Here you sit, after a synagogue has been shot up in Pittsburgh, two African Americans have been gunned down in a Baltimore grocery store, and a series of pipe bombs have been sent to politicians through the post. That is what you should be praying about! How can it make sense to repair a disgusting sheep with a bit of old beaver to satisfy a pathologically obsessive poodle? Why should God possibly be interested in such an idiotic problem? Grow up!*

Pip's paw taps my thigh again, but this time when I look down, understanding seems to dawn on her clever little face. She smiles and rests her head encouragingly on my lap while I struggle to pin the improvised beaver pelt in a way that will yield enough firm surfaces to stitch into. Threading a massive, hooked upholstery needle with the strongest stuff I have—many-stranded lavender silk embroidery floss—I take a stab at attaching beaver to sheep.

It is every bit as tough going as I thought it might be. The matted condition of Ding-y's wool often requires me to lean the back of the needle into the table and push with all my might. I realize that in doing so, I am denting the teak veneer of what has been, over the course of about forty years, a de Vries family dining table, Richard's graduate school desk, our own temporary dining table of seventeen years standing, and now a home for my sewing machine and paint boxes. Pip is not the only one to hold onto scratched and imperfect pieces of the past. It would be pretty hypocritical if I pitched her ancient, plague-riddled sheep into the bin!

A third cup of tea, and the repairs continue. The skeptical voice in my head has grown faint because I am no longer listening. Pip, curled up at my feet, looks happy and relaxed. Feeling better about my absurd task, I devise a pink blindfold to cover Ding-y's eye sockets, since they are clearly a weakness Ciaran might exploit.

The new pup has come upstairs and is rolling upside down on the rug with a half-destroyed Canada Goose in his paws. The crunchy plastic bottle inside it is wonderful! Cir thought Pip might be tantalized by it too when he shoved it in her face a few minutes ago, but he has decided to enjoy it alone. I tie off a thread and pause. The old pup looks up at me as I watch the new one for a few minutes. My shoulder aches, but I'm glad, after all, that I have chosen to redeem the time with Frankensheep this morning. It has been good to see Young Pip lurking in those brown eyes and to remember that Young Lot must still be somewhere inside me. I should invite her out more often. Across the room, feet in the air and wobbling on his back, Young Cir is all there is right now, but the seeds of his becoming are already growing. He is a pain and a love, and I would not be without him. Pip and I exchange smiles. I finish tying Ding-y's bell with a new purple ribbon and hand over the sheep. Pippa's delight warms the room. Cir comes to see what all the fuss is about, is warned off even approaching Ding-a-ling, and returns to his bottle goose. In my heart, a prayer of thanks arises—for small wholenesses in the midst of great brokenness and for the restorative power of a morning spent against my better judgment.

Rebel Without a Cause

~

Meg Bredesen

I have always been called a rebel. From the time I flushed my peas down the toilet when I was three, there was seldom a rule I heard that I didn't make it my life's work to break. Okay—that isn't entirely true. I only break rules that I think are arbitrary, unfair, or stupid. Unfortunately, that is most of them.

There are some rules I haven't broken. I have never used a blow dryer in the bathtub or a curling iron while sleeping. Now those I consider good rules. And yes, they *are* real rules.

The other problem is I think that rules are okay for others to follow but that I am an exception. Anyway, this cavalier attitude has caused me a *lot* of grief! Whenever I told my poor mother about some new scrape I had gotten into, she would heave a deep sigh, call me a "scofflaw" and ask, "What did you do *this* time?" I tried to blame it on pursuing the "greater good," but really it was just fun to see how far I could push the envelope—that is, until I got caught. I could write a book about *that*.

But, honestly, this rebellion thing is becoming a bore. Speaking up for the ungrateful, downtrodden masses and bucking the system have become tiresome. Besides, I have bigger issues these days. I just had my sixtieth birthday. It is something I was completely unprepared for because I never thought I would live this long. As a result, I've sort of lost my place in the grand scheme of things. I'm in this limbo where I am mentally twenty-five but physically feel like a broken-down seventy-five. For example: I hear about a punk rock concert and, there is nothing I want to do more than don a black leather mini and spike heels and jump into a mosh pit, but the reality is I would fall off those heels and get trampled. And if I so much as look at a couple of donuts, they magically leap onto my artificial hips, never to come off again. I bite into a delicious, crisp apple, only to find my dentures stuck fast!

I heard recently that old age isn't a disease—it's an opportunity. I'm not too sure what that actually means, but I thought it sounded cool. Maybe it is a glorified way of saying youth is wasted on the young. Yes, if I had known then what I know now, my life could have been radically different, but it might have been really boring. I mean—what is life without punk rock, spiked heels, and mosh pits?

Would I do it all again? Yeah, probably, if maybe a little less rebelliously. I'd put the cap back on the toothpaste and always put on a new roll of TP. I'd never leave a dirty dish in the sink and always keep my bedroom clean. See: I really learned from my mistakes (well, maybe not the cleaning part, though it *could* happen—in a parallel universe). But I think I've made peace with my old age. This certainly isn't where I thought I would be at sixty, which is dead, so things can only get better. As Accidental Icon says: age is just a number; it's how you show up for it that counts.

So I've had to trade in the spikes for Danskos and runners, the miniskirts for maxis, and mosh pits for orchestra pits. My makeup routine has gone from thirty minutes to five, if I wear it at all (though I *always* wear lipstick.) Life is just a lot simpler. I don't really care if I fit into the box people want to put me in, so I guess I'm still a rebel. And I still don't care if people like it or not.

The Wild Ride

~

June Hayden

As we make our way down the hill from the campground, I close my eyes and inhale the spring air with a sense of anticipation. Today my brother-in-law is going to take Jim, Carissa, and me for a ride in his bass boat. I am excited but also a little nervous. I've never been in a boat before, I can't swim, and I'm afraid of water, but otherwise, it's all good.

We reach the water's edge, where the boat is tied to a tree, and I get my first close-up view of Lake Shelbyville. The water is clear, with only soft ripples glistening in the morning sunlight. I savor the serene setting and smile hesitantly. *This isn't going to be so bad*, I think, hoping to convince myself. *It may actually be fun.*

I step into the boat, fasten the lifejacket, and settle into my seat. Dean unties the boat, and we pull away from land. I keep my eyes fixed on the shoreline. *Now sit back, relax, and enjoy the ride*, I instruct myself. *Don't look at the water—just focus on the land.*

Everything seems to go well until the shoreline diminishes to a narrow strip of distant trees, and I see we are surrounded by water.

There is no escape! I am trapped in the boat! I am instantly gripped with a strangling panic. My throat tightens. I try to swallow but can't. Wild-eyed, I grab for something, anything, to hold on to.

Just take a deep breath, I tell myself, trying to force a gulp of air past my constricted throat muscles and into my oxygen-deprived lungs. *Calm down right now,* my logical left brain demands. *Everything will be okay.* But my right brain, with its danger-sensing radar, isn't so easily convinced.

I now wish I hadn't dropped that swimming class in college. *But remember why you dropped the class,* my left brain reminds me. *You never learned to float.* It shouldn't have been too difficult. After all, even dead things and inanimate objects can float—no skill is required.

Despite my panic, the Ranger continues its course, and we reach the Shelbyville dam at last. I can see dirt and grass, cars on the highway. Dean turns the boat around; I take a deep breath and exhale slowly. Unaware that the lake is actually an eleven-thousand-acre body of water, I suppose we have reached the halfway point and assume we are now embarking on the final leg of our journey.

I start breathing normally, calmed almost instantly by the thought of heading toward the shore. The fear that has clouded my vision is gone, and I can now relax and enjoy the beauty of my surroundings. I begin to wonder what it would be like to drive a boat and start asking questions, which Dean patiently answers. Finally, he asks if I would like to drive.

"Yes, I would love to!" I reply.

He slows the engine, moves out of the driver's seat, and lets me take over. I don't wait for instructions. I have observed there is a lever that makes the boat go. So I grab that lever—I think it's called a throttle—and push it down. All the way!

In one fell swoop, I unleash the fury of 130 horses. The boat leaps up like a wild stallion, dislodging Dean's companion, who comes hurtling to the back of the boat at high speed, scrambling to maintain her balance. The bow of the boat lifts skyward, producing an avalanche of coolers, drinks, sunglasses, and boat cushions. Dean claws through the debris, frantically trying to get back to the wheel. At the back of the boat, Jim and Carissa also struggle to right themselves.

Thrilled by the surge of power, I am now totally fearless, though everyone in the boat is scared speechless and looking several shades paler than we started. Marty, whose last trace of bravado jettisoned with the first powerful thrust of the engine, is now hunkered against the side of the boat, her head hanging overboard.

"I think I'm gonna puke," she moans.

I laugh maniacally, weaving the metallic red and silver boat through the water but never releasing my grip on the throttle. Dean finally manages to get back into his seat beside me. He jerks the wheel, attempting to avoid hitting other boats. The passengers in the other boats look alarmed and bewildered as we pass by. I wave wildly, still cackling like a drunken fool.

Not ready for the ride to end, I'm disappointed when Dean starts directing me to the shore. We dock the boat and I step aground, exhilarated from the day's adventure. The other passengers feebly and solemnly disembark, exhausted from the frightful escapade but grateful to have survived their wild ride.

A Timely Conundrum

~

June Hayden

Time, say the scientists, is a physical property that, much like our bodies, is affected by mass, acceleration, and gravity. As we age, the effects on our bodies become more pronounced. Our mass increases, acceleration decreases, and gravity intensifies; we slow down a little more each year. So why, then, does time keep speeding up?

Fitbit vs. Step Counter

~

Kelly Nicholson

A step counter clipped onto my pants is more accurate than a Fitbit on my wrist because I talk with my hands. However, a Fitbit cannot be accidentally reset by bending over to tie my shoes! Perhaps complete obliviousness about how many steps I take is actually good and will give me more peace of mind!

Tech Savvy ... Not!

~

Denise Schumaker

It all started when I called the internet support 1-800 number to see what I needed to do to get the Wi-Fi to work. I am not computer literate, so I wasn't exactly sure what to ask for. The company representative asked me to turn on my computer and follow instructions as she gave them. After an exchange that seemed long to both of us, the service representative, with frustration mounting in her voice, asked if I had a relative or neighbor close by who could help.

"No, I'm afraid I don't."

"Are you sure you can't find somebody?" She was desperate. Finally, she told me I might have to hardwire the router to the computer. I told her it was hardwired. The computer was so old it didn't use Wi-Fi!

"Good. You don't need Wi-Fi to connect!' She was in a hurry to hang up and emitted a shrill sound to signal how glad she was to be rid of me. I thought that was quite unfair, since she was the one who had told me to go to the computer to begin with.

"Wait," I said loudly, before she could disconnect, "I have other devices that do need Wi-Fi." The representative sighed and asked what they were.

"My cell phone, laptop computer, and Roku TV." She said I would have to connect each device separately, and for that, all I had to do was put in my password! Of course, I didn't have a password for the new router or know where to find one. At this point, I began to wonder if I would ever be able to use my devices again!

But the exhausted company rep came through. She walked me through setting up the cell phone and made sure it was working. I thanked her very much, and, mutually relieved, we hung up, very glad to end our short but intense acquaintance!

So now I know how to connect all my devices to Wi-Fi, and I'm a little more tech savvy than before. Next time I will know what to ask for—maybe! I can just imagine that tech person getting off the phone, giving herself a facepalm, and shaking her head after we hung up. I bet she was thinking I shouldn't be allowed to own a computer. Never mind—she'll get here herself someday!

Washing Dishes

~

Roxanne Frey

After I received my engagement ring and was officially the fiancé of John D. Frey, I informed my future husband that the first appliance we would purchase after we set up housekeeping would be a dishwasher.

Growing up as the oldest of three children, I was given the job of watching my younger siblings every afternoon after we got off the school bus. My father worked in town, but we lived on a farm that still had dairy cows and pigs. My sister is four years younger, and my brother is six years younger. I was almost the third adult in the house, so I was expected to start supper and keep the house from being torn apart. My sister was helpful, but my brother never did do anything I told him to do.

Until the livestock were no longer deemed an essential part of our family's livelihood, I was also in charge of feeding the swine and herding the cows into the barn. When my dad got home from work, he still had to take care of the second round of milking. The first round was done early in the morning before he went to his factory job. Life on the farm was less complicated after the livestock was sold.

Somewhere in the midst of all of those chores, I still managed to do homework and enjoy a few minutes of watching Dick Clark's American Bandstand. My mother would finish fixing supper after she got home from school, where she taught fourth grade. It all worked just fine except for one thing.

After supper, I was still expected to do the dishes. Sometimes I could get my sister to help dry. Occasionally my father pitched in and helped. After supper, my mother was busy grading papers or doing her own homework for college classes required to keep up her certification. She didn't have time to wash dishes, either. My brother was too young, although I often suspected he was pretending he couldn't figure out how to pick up a dish towel and dry a piece of silverware.

All through the last years of elementary school and high school, as long as I was home for the evening, I was the dishwasher. The dishes got done by someone else the nights that I worked as a waitress in town at the local diner. They also seemed to get washed and dried the nights that I was out on a date. For some reason, when I was home, no one else ever appeared to take over the sink and its load of pots, pans, and plates.

When I left for college, I happily told my sister she was next in line to be chief dishwasher. She was learning to cook in her high school home economics classes, so she could start supper and do some other things in the kitchen. I also told her to recruit our brother to be her dryer.

My first year of college was spent at the Carthage College campus the last year it was located in Carthage, IL. After discovering that it was difficult for a freshman to find an empty washing machine in the dorm laundromat, I decided to use my midweek break from classes to drive home to our farm, twelve miles north of Carthage, to do my laundry. My mother agreed to let me use her car, which was sitting in front of her school, just a few blocks from the college.

So about six weeks after school started, I drove home for the first time, wondering if the sink was full of dirty dishes or if my sister had been able to keep up with the task. When I walked into the kitchen, I noticed that the sink was empty. There weren't even any dirty dishes from breakfast. Standing in a corner not far from the sink was a new contraption that hadn't been there before I left for college. It was a brand new General Electric portable dishwasher, already partially full of the dirty dishes from breakfast. I had been replaced by a machine!

I still regard my dishwasher to be my most important appliance. You can have my stove, my refrigerator, my washing machine, and dryer. But you can't take away my dishwasher!

The Dirty Truth About Toilet Paper

~

Meg Bredesen

There are many things in life I find confusing, but one of the most confusing of all is purchasing toilet paper. Every time I buy some, I feel like I need a calculator.

Back in the day, when old Mr. Whipple admonished us not to squeeze the Charmin, it had 500 sheets per roll. Don't ask me how I remember this. I just do. But sure as civilization is in decline, so are the number of sheets on a regular roll of toilet paper. First they puffed up the rolls to make them look bigger; then they started saying they were double, then triple, then jumbo, and now mega. But are they really? I think not!

I recently purchased a package of Charmin Ultra Soft. When I got it home, I discovered that 4 rolls were supposed to equal 24 regular rolls. I was incredulous! How could this be? I brought out my calculator. If each roll has 450 sheets, then we are looking at a package total of 1800 sheets. Divide that by 24 "regular rolls," and it means that each would have just 75 sheets. Even if you peeled the sheets and made the rolls single ply, they'd still only have 150 sheets. In what world is 75 sheets (or even 150) an acceptable roll? In addition, the package says it will fit any TP roller, and I can tell you from personal experience that that is more false advertising!

Then there is Charmin Essentials Strong. I'm not sure what constitutes its strength; is it interwoven with steel mesh? No idea. It also says it is "essential," so I'm wondering where that leaves ordinary Charmin. This one claims it has 300 sheets per roll and that 6 rolls equal 15 regular rolls! Again I do the math and discover that to turn 15 rolls into 6, you'd be looking at just 120 sheets per regular roll.

My last purchase of TP was Angel Soft. It has a cute baby with wings floating on a cloud. This package says that 12 jumbo rolls equal 26 regular rolls…huh? These only have 250 sheets per roll. You get the picture—115.4 per! It also says it's their strongest TP ever, but this marketing claim would be better illustrated if the baby had on a muscle shirt to show off his biceps, or maybe a leather jacket and chains. Just sayin'….

This brings us to generic toilet paper. I recently found a wrapper under my sink for "Psssst" brand. I don't think they really thought this name through. Really? *Psssst*? Anyway, there is no jumbo or mega roll claim, just 250 sheets. Sad to say, and wholly unexpected, Psssst is the winner of my toilet paper challenge. There is no sweet little bear named Skids doing his happy dance because his heinie is clean, no cute, winged baby on a cloud, just 250 honest sheets of Psssst.

I don't know about you, but I'm outraged. How can the cheapest toilet tissue have the largest number of sheets on a regular roll? Something should be done about this fraud being perpetrated on an unsuspecting public. Please join my protest and contact the BBB, the FTC, the ACLU—maybe even the president—and say that we won't stand (or sit) for the lies those dirty chiselers are feeding us. The only way we can make these companies listen is if we hit them where it hurts. I'm calling for a full-on boycott of toilet paper. It's the only way we can show we mean business (#1 or #2). Change *will* happen, but only if we band together. Ban toilet tissue and its dishonest marketing from your home. It's not just TP you're flushing—it's money, advertising integrity, and some other stuff!

Diary of a Pandemic Grandmother

~

Roxanne Frey

My role as a military mom includes serving as backup for childcare in case my son is called up for emergency duty with the Illinois National Guard. As I turned the calendar from 2019 to 2020, I noted that Master Sergeant Frey's March deployment would coincide with spring break on the local school calendar. Smiling at the misnomer for a holiday that astronomically would begin the last week of winter, I blocked seven days on my calendar.

With both of my grandchildren home from preschool and fourth grade, I would be on "grandma duty" from sunup to sundown while my daughter-in-law worked her ten-hour shift at the local hospital. With jackets, we would be warm enough to take a picnic to one of the local parks to spend part of the day. I could survive a week without club meetings and coffee with friends while the grands enjoyed going down slides and swinging on monkey bars.

To prepare for my week with the kids, I moved up an eye appointment and began to fill my grandmother's bag with story books and puzzles. While driving to Champaign to pick up my new glasses, I heard on the radio that all Illinois schools would be closed the last two weeks of March to ward off a possible flu epidemic. Non-essential businesses were ordered to shut their doors. Most disheartening was the news that all public parks and playgrounds would also close.

As I passed the nearly empty parking lot of my favorite plant nursery, I pulled in and grabbed a couple of flats of garden seedlings and some onion sets. My grands and I would trade playground apparatus for garden tools to plant an old-fashioned victory garden in their backyard. If nothing else, we would have pansies to brighten our day and fresh green onions to add zest to our salads.

On a hunch, I added several jars of old coins that needed sorting to my grandma's bag of tricks. My granddaughter couldn't believe the dates on some of the pennies. Each child drew out a penny from the jar, and we used my cell phone to Google a list of historical events for the two years. We asked Alexa to play us the music that was popular in 1943, when my parents were married, and also for 1979, when their father was born. That is how we discovered that things were pretty dire for Americans during WWII, with all kinds of items being rationed, including sugar, shoes, and gasoline. We especially enjoyed dancing to the music of George M. Cohan's *Yankee Doodle Dandy*. Suddenly our deprivations in 2020 didn't seem so dire.

Eventually our penny social studies gave way to a daily online classroom of homework provided by my granddaughter's fourth grade teachers. My grandmotherly instincts to keep the two grands off the computer as much as possible had to give way to Zoom and YouTube school. With the help of email assignments from art and music teachers, I planned activities outside, away from the computer. My nine-year-old showed me how to use my cell phone to record the results, and then send proof of our sidewalk decorations made with homemade chalk paint.

Despite the new style of classroom, old-fashioned things lurking in my closets still managed to provide some links between the past and present. When the music teacher asked his students if a typewriter could be a musical instrument, that was my clue to dig out my old portable typewriter. To my amazement, my granddaughter's keyboarding skills were far more accurate—and speedier—than my own. She spent several afternoons composing a story on the baby blue Royal typewriter, which was manufactured in a plant in Springfield, Missouri, where my aunt and uncle worked after their move there in the late 1950s. In our report to the music teacher, we offered a duet, as I also had my mother's red version of the same brand of typewriter.

Recipes from my electronic cookbook application helped provide cooking lessons and special family dinners. On March 17, we made a green gelatin poke cake that cooled in the refrigerator while the grands enhanced the dinner table with homemade paper shamrocks and brightly colored rainbows.

A few days later, we prepared an after-dinner comedy show. The four-year-old made up his own jokes, which were almost as funny as the ones his sister read out of a book. Their father laughed as he recognized the jokes, read from a paperback retrieved from a shelf of books he had left behind in his old childhood bedroom.

We picked out a country to study and celebrated with an all-things-French dinner complete with French fries, French green beans, and French bread. On another evening, there was a chilly outdoor Earth Day concert held in front of our garden. During one particularly difficult week for their parents, we had a memorable night of using YouTube and a ukulele for a karaoke concert of tunes reminiscent of my son and daughter-in-law's courtship.

After one challenging day when both parents had unexpectedly arrived home earlier than usual, I decided to go straight to my own home without staying for supper. The natural bickering between a brother and sister confined without access to their friends had overwhelmed my patience. Despite my goal to use all of our time together expanding our world beyond the boundaries of our geographic restrictions, I had let the two grands spend the afternoon playing games on their own individual electronic devices. Somehow I felt like I had failed the final exam required for successful grandparenting.

In January, none of us could have ever predicted spring break 2020 would last until September, with the kids blocked from most of their normal activities. As I headed to the car, my grandson looked up from the flowers he was helping his mother water and asked one question that made my spirits soar: "Grandma, why aren't you having dinner with the family?" His question embodied all the purpose that we have for being a family in both good and bad times. We lost a season of juggling soccer, T-ball, and softball schedules with voice and dance recitals. However, we didn't lose our humanity and love for one another.

"The Corona Virus 19 Pandemic and our Hopes" An Acrostic

~

Luz Whittenbarger

Chastised by the virus that constrained us all,

Once vibrant, the world turned to somber with apocalyptic speed,

Routine life was profoundly disrupted by eerie, mournful moods,

Obliterating comforts, pleasures, and blessings of regular routine.

Nature's rhythm unchanged! Rain, sun, and birds' songs welcomed beautiful spring, but

Abandoned businesses, banned social touch, and barren streets are realities of today.

Visions of red-marked maps of the world's desperate nations, disease-ridden with the virus,

Invaded earth's landscapes and held humans under siege,

Rendering all peoples too vulnerable to endure the assault of COVID-19.

Unforeseen fear, suffering, and grief have brought the orb to its knees,

Showing no deference to treasure, color, race, age, or creed.

Heroic work of scientists, health experts, and caregivers working to stop the invader, who

Obstinately reminds us that all humans are created and afflicted the same.

Power of faith and prayers will help us overcome, increasing mankind's hopes and labors,

Ending at last the humbling grip of anguish, exhaustion, distance, death, and tears,

Seeking the return of unmasked faces, dialogue, warm embraces and dreams without fear.

Travel in the Time of Quarantine

~

June Hayden

To say we're excited would be an understatement. The car has been checked, the gas tank is filled, and the tires have been aired. We've had our showers, and we're all ready to set out on our big adventure in the morning. We'll be using Walmart's curbside pickup for the first time. We're buying groceries!

The Shopping List
~
Jacqueline Worden

"Help! Shopping for bargains is such a temptation! But I've checked, and I don't need any footwear, socks, underwear, casual clothes, dressy clothes, winter garb, sketchbooks, journals, pencils, art supplies, bowls, or mugs. I *need* to remember my abundance."

"Dear," my husband said, "just carry a list titled 'What I Need.' It would be blank."

A Tribute

~

Jane Gilbert

She spoke in a soft voice, wore clunky shoes, walked with a limp. She wrote stories about being a hippie in San Francisco, cheering for the Giants, and living with disability. She taught us about the fifty-five-word masterpiece. She was funny and gentle and strong. Her name was Johnni. How we shall miss her!

Nature Walk Surprises

~

Kelly Nicholson

In light of the stay-at-home mandate stemming from COVID-19, I thought nature walks might be a good way to take advantage of the sunshine and get some exercise.

But then I remembered that I'd gone hiking the previous year at Shades State Park in Indiana, where I quickly learned that trail signs labeled *Rugged* should have read *Welcome to Nature Hell, where there's a good chance you'll die.*

I decided to do something a little easier. I'd dust off my digital camera and play amateur photographer, since I hadn't taken many photos since 2016, when the newspaper I worked for closed its doors. I was starting to feel the itch.

Initially I thought of going early in the morning and taking pictures in the light of dawn. But I woke up to fog so dense that I couldn't see the other side of the pond right in front of the house. So I waited until the afternoon, when the fog had burned away and there was no danger of being run over by wildlife in frantic flight from the heavy mist. I set out to explore the family farm with a bottle of water and a walking stick that Dad always called the "bub club."

When I got to the big creek, I realized that starting a photography nature walk at noon was a problem: my digital camera did not have a viewfinder. When I wanted to take a picture, the only option was to look at the digital screen to see what the lens was picking up. Fortunately, I'd had this camera since my junior year of high school: it had seen me through taking pictures for Paris High School's yearbook and newspaper, making memories during college, and covering many stories as a reporter for the Paris Beacon-News.

Even with the direct sunlight preventing me from seeing what was on the screen, I knew how to get good shots by looking at the shadows. I turned my camera to any and every interesting thing: animal tracks, trees, ducks, water.

The movement of the creek and the way the light was reflecting off the water prompted several pictures. I also tried to experiment with focus. I got up close and personal with a stem of thorns and managed to get them in such sharp focus that looking at the image felt like it hurt. The trees and dead leaves came out blurry, allowing the green of the stem to pop.

I spent most of my time off-road in parts of the woods that I'd always driven or walked by. I kept to the well-worn paths my dad and uncle had made over the years, and although I didn't go to extremes exploring, I did find a part of the creek that was the very picture of a babbling brook, but the brush blocked the view, and there was a severe drop right next to it. Along the creek, erosion had taken its toll on the banks, and the tree in front of me was in danger of falling into the water.

As I went about my walk, I realized I'd finished an entire workout without being aware of it, complete with lots of squatting, climbing, and high-stepping over thorns, as I did whatever I needed to do to get my shot without getting hurt.

I made my way up to the house and started to explore around the barn lot west of it. Since it wasn't yet spring, all the areas that normally would be covered in tall grass were easily navigated without worrying about bugs or an animal scaring the dickens out of me.

Exploring those grassy areas, I found a small creek that barely had any water trickling downhill. It was on the other side of some thick stickers and thorns. All along the water's path, vibrant green moss grew among the dead leaves from winter. In the sunlight, the scene looked like a forgotten fairyland. I'd lived all these years on my family's farm, and I had no idea that this place existed!

Soon it was time to head home. I had taken a couple of steps along the creek bed to find a thinner spot in the thorns when my attention was drawn by a sudden rustle of dried leaves. Peeking through the leaves, I saw something scaly and grayish-black curling in front of me. I promptly turned back, bolting through the thorns, saying, "Nope! I'm out of here!"

It wasn't until I got into the grassy area that I realized I had stickers all over me. My legs were stinging from the thorns that had pierced through my yoga pants.

I was done exploring.

A Flash of Wings

~

Amy Lynch

A flash of wings always catches my eye. Even if I don't physically stop what I'm doing, my eyes follow the movement and usually, before the bird lands or flies out of sight, I'll silently identify it as a phoebe or flicker or finch. Sometimes the name that comes to mind will startle me out of whatever I'm doing, and I will stop abruptly to burst out, "I think that is a tanager," or "Could that be a towhee?" When that happens, everything else has to wait until I can decide. My family is patient with these interruptions, and they even work to help me notice birds that they hope will be a novelty. Their kindness prompts them to do so, but I think they also enjoy my enthusiasm, even if they don't quite share it.

This enthusiasm of mine crept up on me, and I'm not sure of the source. My earliest memory of watching birds was during a Rapid City blizzard when I was a child. The drifts were huge and rose above the windows of our lowest floor, mounding snow around the juniper bushes pressed against the panes. Robins had taken refuge inside those sheltering branches and were enclosed in a green world. From inside, we could watch their red breasts and shiny black eyes as they hopped about within the trees, eating an occasional juniper berry. My dad's smile split his face as he stood at the window and said, "Well, how about that?" Those beautiful prisoners only stayed a day before the Rapid City weather pivoted back to spring with a quick thaw and they flew off to eat some cold and confused worms!

Other birds have caught my attention over the years. As graduate students living in downtown Oakland, Doug and I were mesmerized one evening when scores of birds, from pigeons to herons, circled higher and higher overhead, climbing the heat thermals that rose from hot city streets. Our necks grew stiff, but we couldn't tear our eyes away from that column of soaring birds.

I remember family vacations with our children on the Oregon coast, where we'd watch the black-feathered oystercatchers prowl gray rocks and search in crevices for tidbits of food lodged there by the tide. The birds' neon-orange beaks and legs flashed along the rocks almost like disembodied parts.

Gradually, it wasn't just the unusual birds or remarkable avian events that drew my eye. I began to appreciate that I was living in a world full of feathered creatures. Pieces of information kept clicking into place so that I started to be able to decode messages that had previously been secret. Hearing the cries of crows in the distance, I look up to see if they are chasing a hawk or an owl across the sky. If the sound is near my pond, I'll scan the shoreline, looking for a red-shouldered hawk that might have come by to catch a froggy snack. A cheerful ladder of notes in the early morning sends me outdoors to scan the treetops for orioles, and I slice fresh oranges to put out in case they come closer. Doug and I sleep with the window open most of the year, so I can hear the earliest birds singing in the trees outside; every once in a while, we are lucky enough to hear a barred owl in the night calling, "Who cooks for you? Who cooks for you all?"

My mother's birding enthusiasm seemed to grow at the same time as mine, or perhaps I noticed her interest in birds as I discovered my own. On our frequent phone calls, we shared stories about the birds we had seen. She was in the Black Hills of South Dakota, where there were often turkeys and crossbills in the winter. Each spring, we both waited anxiously for tree swallows and mountain bluebirds to nest in the boxes she'd hung on the wooden fence posts along her meadow. Often, Doug and I would visit over spring break and be there to see the first arrivals.

Living in Central Illinois, we had dozens of birds a day in our own yard, and my mother loved to hear stories of robins and yellow-bellied sapsuckers eating bittersweet berries on the vine outside my kitchen window in winter. Later in the year, I shared pictures of goldfinches in the zinnias, catbirds in the mulberry bushes, and cuckoos and tanagers high in the tree canopy, eating tiny green caterpillars. When I discovered that it wasn't just official flycatchers like phoebes and kingbirds that swept through the trees to catch moths on the wing—that cedar waxwings could do so too—I couldn't wait to share the news with her. There was so much to watch right outside my window: nuthatches prying under the shingled flaps of shagbark hickory trunks and kingfishers, along with green and great blue herons, hunting fish in the pond. The stillness of herons was broken by lightning-fast stabs through the water's surface, and the kingfisher's rackety battle cry preceded a splashing dive. Sometimes I was surprised by what seemed to be unlikely meals, like the great blue heron eating a chipmunk that had strayed across its path.

Mom visited us frequently and always noticed our birds. When she and her partner Jim moved to Charleston in 2014, we spent hours together on her deck, watching the birds that filled the yard. Flocks of cardinals and a half dozen woodpeckers were always part of the action, but others required more patience on our part. Eventually we'd hear a rustle in the dead leaves under the hedge and the debate would begin. Were those movements quick enough to be made by a white throated sparrow? If sudden stillness was followed by a haunting song, we knew it could be a thrush turning those leaves, and if they were being tossed out far and wide, we surmised that a brown thrasher was probably using its long, curved beak to root through piles of them at once. Sitting together in the sun, chatting aimlessly, we looked forward to each new season and the chance to see our feathered friends again.

Mom's health declined abruptly in spring 2017, and she spent a few weeks in the hospital. I stopped at her house on my way to visit each morning, because her first question when I arrived was always about whether the feeders and birdbath were filled.

After Mom died, I felt enormously tired and moved through my life at a very slow pace for a long time. Perhaps that was why the birds around me became so calm? Soon after her passing, a normally skittish indigo bunting paused at the feeder that I was about to fill and just watched me. I stood and stared. Eventually the bunting left, but I began to notice that all of the birds seemed to slow down that summer and look at me. Somehow, I got the idea that my mom was borrowing their eyes for a moment and looking out to see how I was doing. I'm sure I could have dissuaded myself of this with a little effort, but why? Instead, I just smiled at them and said, "Hi. How are you? I'm fine. We miss you." The birds seemed to nod and stay a little longer before they took flight.

Day by day and bird by bird, I felt a little better. Now I am happy to let the birds lead me through the seasons, giving me something to enjoy each day and something to look forward to tomorrow.

In the Middle of a Song

~

Naomi Hills

In memory of Rick, lead player for The Spirit Road Band.

When I was three years old, my musical journey began alongside my father, who played guitar and sang with Burl Ives in Terre Haute, Indiana in the 1930s. The first time I saw the smiles on people's faces while I was singing, I realized that this was what I was meant to do.

I was an only child living in a big farmhouse in the country and singing to the chickens. They were my first big audience. Every day, I stood in the chicken house on a wooden egg bucket for my stage, with a hairbrush for a microphone. The chickens were a captive audience, but I don't remember them smiling! Mother would always say it was no wonder they didn't lay any eggs, which was probably true.

When I was much, much older, I organized The Spirit Road Band, and we traveled through thirty-three states and parts of Canada. I had many "brothers in music," as I called them. I remember one especially, whose time on stage was cut way too short. It was just like he left in the middle of a song. Rick was also three years old when he began singing and playing guitar. He didn't have a lot of material things, but his love of music seemed to be enough for him. He played for more than seven years in The Spirit Road Band, and the way he moved those strings always brought a big hand.

Now Rick's guitar sits silent in a lonely, dark room, waiting for its master to come back soon, but the one who ruled those strings no longer plays and sings. He left the stage in the middle of his song.

Silence

~

Stacy Lynn

The radio scratches in my ears, and from the back seat, I can just make out the count of balls and strikes through the AM static. My little sister is next to me in the back seat, jabbering to my mom, who is in the front passenger seat, her head turned around, jabbering back at my sister. I have no idea what they are saying, and I do not care. I am trying to read my book.

My dad is driving and smoking and keeping a scorecard. The car windows are cracked open to keep us from choking to death. The wind noise is crashing into the radio static, occasionally mixing with the sudden clarity of the radio signal and the baseball announcer calling a play at the plate. My dad curses and bangs his fists on the steering wheel: the Reds are losing. Still, I am trying to read, dammit, and we have another baseball game's worth of driving; I am losing my mind in the chaos. Can't the quiet of my book overcome us all? What would be the cost of one hour of silence in this car? What could I pay them to whisper? Why is there always radio static and sisters and Mom jabbering and wind noise and Dad yelling at baseball games?

Today, I live alone. Silence is a precious joy in my life, treasured, filled up with reading one book after another, with *New Yorker* magazines sprinkled in between. Oh my goodness, the quiet is divine. Yet there are days when I would trade in all of my books and my solitude for one hour in the back seat of the car with the chaos of my childhood. Hearing my mom and sister jabbering away, my mind unsettled by the wind noise and the Reds playing on the radio, while my dad curses the blown call at the plate.

Just a Little Off-Key

~

Bill Heyduck

When I was in fifth grade, my parents had an old upright piano given to them. I wondered why they brought it home, because neither of them played any musical instruments. My mother had played the violin as a child, but her interest was short-lived, and the violin went to the attic for the next sixty years. After the piano was delivered, my two siblings and I tried to play music, but we mostly just made discordant noise, plinking on the yellowed ivory keys.

The following fall, my mother asked me if I would like to take piano lessons. I was surprised but agreed that it sounded like fun. Mom said the WPA music teacher would be traveling from school to school, and lessons would to be offered at the Garfield School, which I attended. They would be group lessons once a week during lunch hour and would cost twenty-five cents a lesson.

There were five squirming sixth graders waiting that first day for our introduction to the piano. This lunch hour lesson was a tight fit into my schedule. I had to run about five blocks home, eat,

191

and return for the lesson in thirty minutes. That left thirty minutes for the five of us to receive our individual instruction.

At the first class meeting, the teacher introduced us to the keyboard and showed us which notes on a sheet of music matched which keys on the piano. That sounded simple enough to me. After this introduction, we were each presented with a little book of simple songs. The songbook cost an extra ten cents. I was afraid Mom was going to think the lessons were getting a little too expensive.

The teacher played through each song for us, pointing out the matching notes and keys, which we mimicked with fumbling fingers. The half hour was up, and we were told to report back next week, prepared to play the music we were given. We were each sternly warned to practice.

The first week passed, and when we met for our lesson, each of us stumbled through our pieces. The teacher pointed out our mistakes and sent us home to practice. With five students and thirty minutes for teaching divided among the group, progress was slow. I became bored playing the same tune over and over and decided to compose a song of my own.

It was easier to remember notes that I had written myself. I could whiz through the simple composition without missing a beat. I thought that at the next lesson, I would surprise the teacher with something original.

The day of the lesson arrived, and I fidgeted and squirmed until it was my turn to play. I sat by the teacher, reached a sweaty hand into my pocket, and pulled out a wrinkled piece of paper with the notes of my song correctly located on a hand-drawn musical staff. I informed the teacher it was my own original composition and that I wanted to play it for her.

She didn't bat an eye; she simply snatched the wrinkled paper out of my hand, saying I should spend my time practicing the lesson she had provided and not waste her time doing things I didn't know anything about. I was crushed; I had waited all week to perform my song for her. My interest in learning to play the piano took a sudden plunge.

The piano at home didn't help my musical advancement. Not only was it out of tune (we couldn't afford to have it tuned), but my younger brother had walked on the keys and even jumped up and down on them; I caught him in the act. The result of this abuse was the death of some keys. About one-third of the keys, when pressed, came out as a thud and not the expected musical tone. It totally upset the rhythm and the tonal quality of what I was trying to achieve. Practice became a frustrating, irritating experience, and I avoided it at every opportunity.

The lack of practice was my undoing because the dreaded Christmas recital was suddenly upon me. With much misgiving, but firmly pulled along by my mother, I arrived at the recital location. I was about the eighth student to perform. By the time I sat at the piano, my hands were dripping with sweat. As I played, my sweaty fingers seemed to slip off the intended keys and onto the adjoining ones.

After what seemed like an eternity, I reached the last note. With my head bowed, I slipped back and sat beside my mother and wanted to disappear. On the way home, Mom kindly suggested that since the piano was so out of tune, maybe I should give up my music lessons. I wanted to shout for joy, but I restrained myself and only nodded my agreement.

Photograph of bearer

ADMITTED
JUN 28 1959
Mrs. B. MATZ SERVICE
NEW YORK N.Y. 15

CLASS
TO

4

This passport is valid only for use in connection with the bearer's residence abroad as a dependent of a member of the American Military or Naval Forces or a dependent of a civilian employee of the Government on active duty outside the continental limits of the United States.

This passport, unless limited to a shorter period, is valid for two years from date of issue. It may be renewed but the final date of expiration shall not be more than four years from the original date of issue.

5

An Ocean Voyage

~

Julie Rea

O ur family of five was returning to Germany for the second
time as assigned by the armed forces. My father drove us
from Fort Knox to New York City via the Shenandoah
Valley where we visited my mother's people before leaving the
country for three and a half years.

It was late winter of 1956 when we boarded the S. S. Buckner
docked at New York's harbor and it would take us over a week to
sail the Atlantic to the German port of Bremerhaven. We three
children settled on board quickly, looking forward to the adventure
as we had on previous ocean journeys.

During past trips, I spent hours on deck, hanging over the
railing, soaking in the smells. colors and sounds of the ocean
waves as the big boat cut through the water. This trip, maybe not
so much.

Daytimes we dressed casually for ease of movement and
comfort. After a couple of days, my mother insisted we girls dress
up for dinner. This meant a full cotton skirt over a crinoline, my
blouse held in by my favorite, and only blue cinch belt. My white

bobby socks were pulled high out of my saddle shoes and up under my skirt to hide the fact that I wasn't allowed to shave my legs yet.

Mama said my legs were skinny enough and would look even thinner and too white, so no shaving! She also didn't think I was ready for a bra. A mother's logic...sigh. Needless to say, I was sure I stood out among my peers. Painfully shy, I was not aware of my other appealing features: thick, dark, shiny hair curled into a bob and blue eyes with fair skin.

So one evening I was sitting alone, dressed and groomed, in the ship's lounge waiting for dinner with the family. I hoped and believed I was invisible, but at the same time I thought it would be nice to make a friend. Fate intervened. I was brought out of my self-absorbed reverie by a sudden awareness of others standing close by. Looking up, I met the eyes of a young fellow around my age and a mother type of person right there in front of me.

The young man introduced himself and his mother and asked if I would like to see the movie with him after dinner. These two were both so gentle and kindly mannered that I nodded my head and said, "yes" without another thought. Will glanced at his mother, she disappeared, and he sat down with me. We talked until we each had to join our families at assigned tables.

Will and I kept steady company for the rest of the voyage. We roamed the ship, shared chocolate sodas in the snack bar and enjoyed many a game of ping pong: the only game I was any good at. Later I discovered an aptitude for fencing, but that's another story. Ping pong was fun and challenging for both of us; depending on whether the ship was rolling side to side or end to end.

We never missed the nightly movie in the ship's meeting room that had been converted to a theater. I remember enjoying easy company with a young man I cannot picture clearly now, beyond my general certainty that he had a pleasant physical appearance and an easy, companionable manner. Nor do I recall goodbyes before we disembarked at Bremerhaven. He and his family went their way and I and my family went on to Frankfurt, where I would finish eighth grade.

Looking back, as I am bound to do, I recognize that I had indeed enjoyed successful companionship with a fellow for a time, in spite of the fact that I went on to have four years of barren love life in high school. Surely it would have done my self-esteem some good to have recalled that ship board experience going forward! From fifteen to seventeen I still looked like I was eleven or twelve: I "bloomed" at a turtle's pace.

Now, many years later, I wonder fondly if Will is still out there somewhere? If so, how is he? What has his life been? In any case, I wish him well. I wish him well.

Water

~

Richard England

1) **Miniwanka and Chaos**

We sing R. Murray Schafer's "Miniwanka" with enthusiasm and a sense of unease. It is beautiful but weird. The music marked with our numbers has no conventional notation—no bars or measures—but a new language of musical invention. We begin in unison, a capella: "The wise man delights in water."

Repeated harmonies gradually accumulate, and finally we are just singing the word "water" in half-coordinated, overlapping parts before we begin to interrupt it with the joyfully random peeps and chirps scattered over the page as the unscored score begins to reveal its deep strangeness.

To the young teens whose voices make this music, the whole thing seems by turns exhilarating and absurd. It is clearly alien from our more conventional repertoire. Palestrina has more in common with The Human League, Poulenc with Survivor, than any of them do with this. We mock the piece by inventing gibberish parodies on the carpool rides back to the suburbs after rehearsals, but it remains one of our favorites.

As children, we delight in water in our own ways. At a choir camp, for instance, on the shores of Lake Couchiching, we engage in unauthorized water battles in canoes, splashing, maneuvering, colliding, shrieking, and laughing as water begins to rise in a holed and sinking vessel. As this is all of a dozen yards out, the only modest danger is from the wrath of the camp counselor, a slightly older teen, yelling at us from the wooded shoreline. The lake is chaos and relief from the discipline of singing, and the water is delightful—although it is foolish delight—as we riot in borrowed boats.

2) Water at the Top of the World

From Edmonton to Resolute, you take a commercial jet. At Resolute, you wait a day or two for a window in the weather and sort your gear. From Resolute to Eureka, you take a Twin Otter, a loud, high-winged workhorse of flight wherever runways are short or improvised. Eureka's a military base, so its runway is long, but it's just a stop on the way north of 80.

Once we're refueled, we repack the plane to take one of two teams out and continue north to Disraeli Fjord: three passengers, a skidoo, a few weeks' worth of supplies. The high Arctic is rock and ice, a desert of deep reds and dark greens shot through with fields and veins of brilliant white and blue. The glaciers that shroud worn mountains shoot frozen, shattering tongues out into the sea, where they tumble into a jagged field of floes. From a few thousand feet up, it is impossible to guess their size. It is another world and making sense of it is impossible. You just sit in the plane, numbed by the roar of the engines, awed by the wild and unfamiliar surface you are about to fall onto.

The Twin lands on the snow and smooth ice of Disraeli Fjord, disgorges you, your colleagues, and your gear; then turns, and its deafening presence lifts into the vast blue above, only to slowly dissolve, becoming first a dot, and then a diminuendoing hum that lasts until you can't tell whether you can still hear it or whether you just think you can.

Anyway, if you are interested, this is how you get to the top of the world.

I was eighteen and a field assistant to a geomorphology student who was there to research the interplay of rock and ice in the last few dozen millennia, and our first order of business was to sample the mud of the fjord bed. We did this by drilling through the frozen sea, sending down a coring tube on a thin steel cable, and hauling it back up with the skidoo. It was cold; the ice was eight feet thick, topped with four inches of melt water beneath a foot or so of snow. We suffered for science, gathering clues about how much glacier there had been fifty thousand years earlier, secrets trapped in silt and darkness before our ancestors had decided to start history. The size of glaciers, the age of clay, the depth of the unseen ocean—we sought to fathom what seemed unfathomable.

At the end of the trip we were on Ward Hunt Island, a tiny jumping off point for polar expeditions and Cold War surveillance missions. It sits in the mouth of Disraeli Fjord, with nothing between it and Russia but white polar ocean. Ward Hunt was a mess. There we were, on an island hundreds of kilometers from any human settlement, and we were camped next to a dump. Hundreds of old jet fuel barrels rotted next to the runway; old snow machines had rusted and sank into the permafrost; prefab huts of more modern adventurers had been looted by bears and wolves. I stopped by the station left behind by a recent British team that had unsuccessfully tried to motorcycle their way to the North Pole, and I was horrified to find dozens of torn bags of sliced white bread spilled across the tundra. The little lake where we had hoped to get our water was a no-go zone, its frigid surface shining with oily iridescence. Here, the grandeur of an Arctic Eden had been broken by human purposes and needs. The litter in this frozen desert would last for centuries thanks to the cold, long after the would-be polar motorcyclists were dead. The wise man delights in water, but fools come along and poison it.

3) "Twenty-Three!"

She would always say it in a silly voice, usually from the back of the tour bus. Not quite forty years later, I remember Ann Marie—

blond, curly-haired, and ridiculously cheerful. We were not particular friends but fellow choristers and veterans of the Wales trip ensemble of thirty-six young singers, shouting out our numbers on buses and train platforms, singing pure harmonies in Gothic cathedrals and Victorian concert halls.

Once we grew up and left the choir, I saw Ann Marie maybe once a year when we alumni gathered to sing carols in the postmodern lobby of Roy Thomson Hall before the Christmas concerts of the children's choir, which now seemed a mass of impossibly young and silly things. We older children chatted briefly and reminisced before separating into parts to produce a well-modulated SATB version of "Good King Wenceslas." Our part in the chorus was over, really, and we were reminded of past acquaintances very infrequently.

When she was in her early twenties, Ann Marie took a mountain hike one October day and did not come back. There was a search, but the weather turned: it snowed and stayed cold. The search parties kept searching as days became weeks, and as we read about it in the papers, we worried. Was she alive? Had she been abducted? She was young and beautiful and gone, and unpleasant fears whispered in the void of the unknown. We could only fear and wonder, send sympathies, perhaps pray.

They found her in spring, when the snow melted from the edge of the glacier that had held her through the long mountain winter. She had fallen on the ice, broken a leg, and succumbed to the cold night, shrouded in the first snow. For a little while, she had become part of the glacier she had fallen down while traversing. It was a little comfort to those who loved her, who had known her, that she had been a victim of misfortune rather than human evil.

At the memorial service that summer, I was one of hundreds from the choir or school or her small town or university. There were songs, tears, words, all wrung from the mingled emotions of grief and confusion that follow a delayed closure. I did not know what to think in that packed neo-Gothic Ontario church. Had any of this been God's will? Were all of us twenty-somethings simply lucky? A missed trail, bad weather, and then...what was living even for? While we had been worrying about her fate, she had been snowbound, icebound, a tiny part of a winter glacier. The same ice I had walked up north had killed her out west. The glaciers that spread and shrank, reshaped continents, carved out valleys and hollows—they did so in human hearts as well as rock. Where were the geomorphologists of fate and feeling who could make sense of events that were not adapted to human desires? The priests tried, but despite their good will, they did not seem to help us. No delight in water, just an unsung death.

4) Coda

I think back to "Miniwanka," to the wise man and water. How odd that music was; how little sense it made, and yet it was glorious in its strangeness. I am glad to have sung it, even though we did not really appreciate it, even though I do not listen to it now. We were just children having fun, awed at the beauty of the music we made, which was always present at the edge of our consciousness. The past flows through us like ice through mountains, like music through children, like water remembered in its various shapes. We keep imagining, traveling miles to sink a sampling tube into clay, trying to fathom the stream of events that have gone before, the splendor beyond our normal scales, the deaths that wait for us, outside of our childish understanding.

Last night I listened once more to "Miniwanka." How odd that I should not have remembered the long diminuendo of its last line—"Water never dies. ..."

Now I Remember

~

Jane Gilbert

I think a lot about memory loss these days. Call it Alzheimer's or Lewy body disease or simply generic dementia—more and more people I know or know about are feeling its effects, and I worry about my own increasingly frequent memory lapses. I have watched friends gradually fade away from view, robbed of personality and any sort of meaningful life by memory loss. I know others serving as their caregivers. The loss of memory is more frightening than death. Few of us welcome death, but it seems somehow cleaner than this living death. The person we knew is gone, but the shell is still around to be cared for, grieved over, and perhaps pitied by others.

When someone you love loses their memory, your loss is the same as if the person has died: you've lost not only their companionship but also your joint history. You can no longer go to them and say, "Honey, do you remember that gorgeous sunset, the last night of our Alaskan cruise?" or "Dad, didn't we have some great backyard picnics when I was a kid?" The person who shares those memories with you is gone, and nobody else remembers. Or cares. You've lost part of your life story. Not the big stuff, but the little stuff, the stuff that makes your life so rich. That's where memoir writing comes in.

I can't describe the pleasure, the joy I have received from writing down my memories in the past ten years. I've enjoyed writing all my life, but I decided early on that I could never be a professional author. I don't have the imagination to write fiction, and I don't have the temperament to be a reporter. But with memoirs, you only have to write about yourself, and on that subject I am an expert.

I lost my parents twenty-five years ago. I can no longer go to them and say, "Remember when I almost drowned at the beach when I was five?" or "Remember how you teased me about that awful poem I wrote?" But I can write about those things, and I have. I lost my husband fifteen years ago. I can't say to him, "If you hadn't been so crabby that day, I would have missed that wonderful piece of blueberry pie" or "Do you need that really soft sweater I gave you? I think I'll wear it myself tonight." But I can write about those things, and I have. I enjoy the memories as I write them and as I go back occasionally and reread them. Sometimes I share them with other people who may or may not enjoy them, but that doesn't matter. I am preserving my history for me, not for them.

These writings are not my whole life story. But they are a part of that story. I don't kid myself that they are important in the grand scheme of things, but I like to think that maybe someday, one of my grandchildren or still-unborn great-grandchildren will look at them and find something of interest. Or maybe not. Right now, the pleasure they bring me is enough.

Author

Biographies

PHYLLIS BAYLES:

I was raised as a child of two cultures—American and Greek. Customs, religion, family, and language have impacted my entire life. Past~Forward provided me the motivation to write my experiences. My past helps me understand myself. It explains why I react to events in my life and helps me make decisions. It comforts and guides me. There were, and still are, struggles and defeat, joy and sadness, but both the past and present make me what I am.

I write in hopes readers will be inspired to make their own memories and share them with their families and friends. If they do that, I guarantee the circle of valued memories will widen. Memoirs are stories, but they are also history. When you read a memoir, you're looking at the history of that time.

My husband Eric and I live in Charleston, Illinois. He encouraged me to join Past~Forward and begin writing memoirs. That guy sure knew what good friends, camaraderie, and joy the group would bring to me! It's also been my pleasure to serve as emcee for our public readings.

"Just like us, the older memories grow, the more valuable they become." Mark Chapman, *Senior Living*

MEG BREDESEN:

People always say that the daughters of policemen and ministers are the worst. At sixteen I ran away to Florida for six months, then spent thirty years in California. I came to Illinois in 2018 to be with my mother. Since I arrived two years ago, I have had lots of repairs done—an oophorectomy, arthroscopic knee surgery, two hip replacements, and now a laminectomy on L3 and L4! I share my life with a feisty little dog named Ginger who certainly has a mind of her own, so now I know how my mother felt dealing with me. I joined Past~Forward two years ago and like to write because I enjoy making people laugh and seeing how far I can push the envelope.

MARGIE CHECKLEY:

I was born at home in Mattoon, Illinois, the seventh in a family of eight. I attended Mattoon schools and graduated from Mattoon Senior High. All my life I had a desire to be a professional dancer—I took ballroom dancing for about nine years. I still have a love of dance. I also enjoy poetry as well as writing, and at one point I started making my own greeting cards for different occasions. I graduated from Eastern Illinois University in 1989 and worked at EIU's Booth Library for thirty-six years, retiring in 2003. I was married to John J. Checkley for fifty-one years and blessed with three daughters: Kimberly, Jill, and Mara. John passed away in 2013 and Mara in 2017, both of cancer. I am blessed with wonderful neighbors, friends, and co-workers. I have a sister in Arthur and a brother in North Carolina and many nieces and nephews, as well as great-nieces and great-nephews.

SHELLEY REA CROUCH:

I have been happily married for thirty-six years to John Crouch, a farmer and singer-songwriter. We live in Casey, Illinois, the home of 2,700 people and twelve of the world's largest things.

I am the proud mother of three grown children and am a doting grandmother to a precious granddaughter. I am a semi-retired bookkeeper, homemaker, and home educator, currently teaching English as a second language online part-time to students in China and pursuing my hobbies. I like to write, and I have an idea for a grade school chapter book. I joined the Past~Forward Memoir Writing Group both to improve my writing skills and to spend more time with my mom, who was in the group until her passing. I started learning watercolor painting after her death, and I now aspire to add watercolor illustrations to children's books for my granddaughter. I also enjoy genealogy and would love to write our family history in story form someday. I also enjoy playing the ukulele, and I am learning to play the bass guitar. If such a thing were possible, I would love to learn how to have a beautiful singing voice.

LOIS DICKENSON:

I started reading at age three and never stopped. With training in both history and library science, I devour book content from light romance to sci-fi to historical tomes and scientific treatises as my whims take me. Writing is a natural outgrowth of my love for words and ideas.

I am a part-time genealogist (both researcher and occasional teacher), an amateur artist (more experimental than trained) and a more than decent photographer. I am also a bit of a magpie, picking up shiny objects or mysterious mechanisms just because I like their shape or the way they hint at some interesting backstory. My magpie stash currently resides on my otherwise unused dining room table.

HANNAH EADS:

I consider myself to be an artist/teacher and an amateur writer. During the pandemic year, I have been painting watercolor portraits of flowers as well as continuing to write family stories and accounts of my world travels. My education includes a bachelor's and a master's degree in art from Eastern Illinois University, postgraduate art courses from the University of Illinois, and a doctorate in art education from Illinois State University.

My teaching career began in 1954, and I retired as a professor of art from EIU in 1991. My paintings have been shown in local, state, and regional art exhibitions since 1950. My years of research into my family ancestry led me to the completion of an online course at the University of Toronto, where I earned a certificate in genealogical studies.

I would like to give credit to our Past~Forward memoir group for motivating me to write. Some of my family stories were included in the group's two previous books, *Occasional Writers* and *The Memory Pool*.

CHARLOTTE ENGLAND:

I came to Charleston with my husband Richard in 2013 from the Eastern Shore of Maryland via Pennsylvania, Vermont, and Ontario. My parents were Dutch immigrants who came to Canada in 1955, and from them, I seem to have inherited the condition of frequently being a stranger in a strange land, making new homes and selves along the way. So far in Illinois, I have been a dog training assistant, a Sunday school teacher, a part-time lecturer in English literature at EIU, head of the local arts council, and an aspiring writer of creative nonfiction. Among my joys are my unruly garden, my clever and beloved poodles, a kind and eccentric husband who makes me laugh, and the monthly Past~Forward meetings, where terrific people share the stories of their lives.

RICHARD ENGLAND:

I am dean of the Sandra and Jack Pine Honors College and professor of philosophy at Eastern Illinois University. I read mysteries, short stories, and the *Times Literary Supplement*. I identify as a Manx-Canadian WASO (White Anglo-Saxon Orthodox) and enjoy dog-walking, conversations with students, and charades, as well as occasional lapses into poetry. I do not enjoy grading, email, or writing in first person (he said mischievously).

ROXANNE FREY:

Most of the time, I would rather write than eat. At first light, I start the coffee pot. On a day with no place to go, I fire up the computer and start typing. I work best with bare feet under a dining room table, using both leaves so it will hold my computer along with all of my research materials. Kicking off my shoes, I sift the sands of time through my mind for inspiration. I write and rewrite poems, short stories, and letters.

Writing offers the same calm and joy as walking along a sandy shore. Places where I have dipped my toes in the water and sampled the local beaches with my bare feet include the Mississippi River, the Great Lakes, the Pacific and Atlantic Oceans, and the Mediterranean Sea. As I wiggle my toes under my table, I can almost hear the waves lapping on the shore while I dream of future opportunities. There are plenty of beaches I still plan to explore. No swimming—just walking and composing lines for new stories.

MARTY GABRIEL:

I am the elder of two siblings. Our parents were the emotionally scarred children of immigrants. They survived the Great Depression and prioritized financial security, education, and athletics. They worked hard and became successful professionals. My brother married at a young age, became a wealthy, Bible-thumping CPA, and eventually moved to Florida. I majored in philosophy and played baseball and football at Dartmouth College before teaching and coaching for several years in the Chicago area, where I grew up. Then I got an MSW degree and worked as a school social worker in Chicago for twenty-five years.

I have prioritized play and personal development. Habitually honest introspection, diligent study, and impassioned competitive endeavors involving games of one sort or another are all things I've long valued greatly. Yet emotional intimacy scared me well into adulthood. My life changed dramatically when I left bachelorhood at fifty-one, shortly after my bride, the benevolent, lovely, and wise Daiva Markelis, had embarked on a new career as an English professor at EIU. I have lived very happily with my spouse/muse in Charleston since 2005.

JANE GILBERT:

Over ten years ago, I attended a meeting where I knew very few people and sat down next to a stranger. She introduced herself as Janet and started telling me about a new group being organized in Charleston. A few people had taken a course on memoir writing with the Academy of Lifelong Learning, but after the course was over, they all quit writing despite good intentions.

So Janet and a couple of others decided to start a memoir writing group that would meet regularly to keep themselves motivated. I knew immediately that I wanted to be part of their group. I didn't know then how it would change my life.

As a result of that encounter, I have had hours of enjoyment from writing, rewriting, and sharing what I've written. I have connected in new ways with family as I revisited my life and wrote about it. I have participated in readings for the public and in the publication of three books of memoirs. And I have made a whole new group of friends who have shared their writings with me and encouraged me in mine.

Thank you, Janet Messenger.

JUNE HAYDEN:

I reside just outside Greenup, Illinois with my husband of almost fifty years and a clowder of cats who allow us to live in their home on the condition we keep their food and water pans filled and their litter pans emptied. They often reward us with an affectionate nuzzle or a relaxing snuggle. It seems a fair enough deal to us.

We are parents of an adult daughter; she and her husband have blessed us with the best gift ever—a charming, loving, brilliant granddaughter who is the joy of our lives.

In January 2016, I made a career change that I've never regretted. After twenty-six years in banking, I walked away from the world of finance and joined the company of Happily Retired. The following year, I started attending Past~Forward meetings. What an awesome group! All the members are warm, welcoming, and encouraging.

Because of the pandemic, I've spent a lot of time at home lately. Most days, if I'm not in the kitchen trying out new recipes and taking pictures of my creations, I'm at my computer, writing about my latest kitchen adventure/disaster and later sharing the pictures and stories on social media. Life is good.

BILL HEYDUCK:

I was born in Centralia, Illinois on September 7, 1928, and grew up in Decatur. I have written over forty stories about my life as it passed through the Great Depression, grade school, World War Two, high school, four years in the Marine Corps, the Korean War, seven-plus years of college.

I was happily married sixty-three years to the same woman, as well as fathering two children, teaching art in public schools for twelve years, teaching college ceramics for twenty-nine years, and running my own ceramics business for fifty years.

I now write mostly fiction and published my first novel, *Jacob's Promise*, in May of 2020, with a second novel, *Mosie*, pending publication.

NAOMI HILLS:

I learned early in life that something written from your heart means more than a store-bought gift, so over the years, I've given many of my writings to others. This was my gift to our grandson Adam when he graduated from Purdue University.

Yesterday

It seems when you were small,
not so big and not so tall,
I'd close my eyes and see you play—
but that was yesterday.
Walking down our lane,
I held out my hand and called your name.
Your hand in mine seemed so small.
I'd help you up if you would fall.
Let's go fishing, Grandpy would say—
this I recalled from yesterday.
Today, Grandson, I'm proud of you,
of all the things you say and do.
I'll love you 'til my day is done.
I'm grateful you are my grandson.
Your journey may lead you far away,
but in my heart, it's yesterday.
Graduation is here—this is your day.
Soon you'll be on your way.
You were a boy, and now you're a man.
You can be whatever you want to be,
I know you can.
There's just one more thing I want to say—
I've loved you to the moon and back
Today and yesterday.

Love, Grammy

DONNA KARBASSIOON:

I was born and raised in Kansas, the Sunflower State. I also knew Dorothy—not the one you are thinking of from *The Wizard of Oz*, but my mother! I can proudly say I am a Jayhawker. I graduated from the University of Kansas, where I studied English and French. My father, Ernie, was the first person to tell me that learning another language was an excellent idea.

I started my married life in Lincoln, Nebraska with a young man from the other side of the world. Ebi and I met at KU, and it has been a beautiful journey. We have two boys, one born a Nebraska Cornhusker and one born an Eastern Illinois Panther. Both live right here in Charleston. We have four beautiful grandchildren.

I have always been interested in learning different languages and have learned to speak my husband's language, Farsi. Also, I studied Chinese for a year. We like to travel and knowing these languages has opened the doors to learning about other cultures. I spent seven years as a tutor teaching English as a second language. I aspire to write a book about my life, since I have been living with two cultures for many years.

When I brought up this idea to a dear friend of mine, she said you need to start writing first. As a result, I began participating in several writing groups. I have learned a great deal by beginning to write my memoirs, mostly memories from childhood. I must thank Jane Gilbert for getting me involved in these writing activities. I credit her with being my inspiration to take writing more seriously.

RAYMA LAUGHLIN:

Becoming a writer snuck up on me. After teaching high school English for four years, I stayed home with our children before returning to work. My unexpected adjunct teaching job at a community college led to tutoring at their writing center. Writing for the center's newsletter and contributing for eight years to a regular Christian feature in a suburban St. Louis journal led me along the writing path, especially as it related to faith in Christ.

I was encouraged to start a blog, *lovethatpersists* (not my idea), in 2013 when the journal folded. Moving to Charleston five years ago and joining the memoir groups furthered my motivation and enjoyable education in writing.

Fast-forward to 2020—for Mother's Day, our son and daughter bought a "magic picture frame," or so it seems to me. Each family of three sends pictures to a website, and magically, they appear on my frame.

Seeing our son's wife and daughter on outings to patches of beachfront along Lake Michigan made me miss them even more— I also miss the soothing effects of the sight and sound of water. Family has always been central to me, making my husband's sudden death just three years ago even more difficult.

AMY LYNCH:

I am a retired college administrator and live with my husband, Doug Klarup. We've made our home in Charleston, Illinois for the past twenty-five years. I am an amateur photographer and an avid birder, but my most creative activity is the memoir writing I've done with the evening Past~Forward group. These meetings have been a high point of my month for many years, and I'm honored to be included in this collection.

DAIVA MARKELIS:

I am a writer and professor emerita of English at Eastern Illinois University, where I used to teach creative writing, women's memoir, and various courses on language and linguistics.

My PhD is from the University of Illinois at Chicago in English, with a specialization in language, literacy, and rhetoric. My MA is also in English, with a specialization in creative writing, specifically fiction. My short stories and personal essays have appeared in the *New Ohio Review, Cream City Review*, the *Chicago Tribune, Other Voices, The Rumpus, Crab Orchard Review*, the *Oyez Review, PANK, The Fourth River, Prairie Schooner, Verdad*, and many others. Two have been nominated for the Pushcart Prize. My memoir, *White Field, Black Sheep: A Lithuanian-American Life*, was published by the University of Chicago Press. In my free time, I like to garden, quilt, knit, and watch White Sox baseball. I'm married to the marvelous Marty Gabriel. We are both from the Chicago area and have found unexpected contentment living among the cornfields of Central Illinois.

STACY LYNN:

I am a scholarly editor and historian by day and a writer, voracious reader, and practitioner of yoga by night. Rebuilding my life in middle age, I find comfort in writing and reading and the healing power of words. As a memoirist and wannabe poet, I see words as my path to solace and to truth. Words have the power to give voice and reason to the twisted knots of my grief, which sometime threaten to untether me from my life and the beautiful world around me. I am currently curating my own peace and growing new roots in the earth in a charming 1919 bungalow in Charleston, Illinois, where I live in the company of my two beloved dogs, Dr. Pepper and Miss Bug.

JANET MESSENGER:

In 2008, I planned to start writing a family history that would be shared with relatives and passed on to future generations. I needed help with the project and was fortunate to find that EIU's Academy of Lifelong Learning offered an Introduction to Memoir Writing class.

It was my lucky day when I met the instructor, Dr. Daiva Markelis, and the six adults who would be my classmates. We learned aging had benefits—the older you were, the more experiences you had to write about. And learn we did—from each other and by writing and sharing our interests, varied backgrounds, and experiences. When the course ended, we planned to go forth and write but soon discovered that without the support and encouragement of our fellow writers, we failed to write much.

Later we regrouped with plans to form a memoir writing group that would welcome others in the community interested in writing, so we began the Past~Forward Memoir Writing Group. Fast forward to 2020: we now have two groups, day and evening, that meet monthly. Both welcome new writers. I've had the privilege of coordinating the activities of the day group, and Daiva leads the evening sessions.

As for the family history I began twelve years ago, it continues as a work in progress. I've also enjoyed writing about my dog, Milo, who took on a personality and voice of his own. You'll find a couple of his adventures in this book.

KELLY NICHOLSON:

After becoming an Eastern Illinois University Panther in 2010, I started working on my bachelor's degree in English. During a class with Dr. Daiva Markelis, I heard about the Past~Forward Memoir Writing Group, and, four years after graduation, I joined the group.

Despite claiming I would never be a journalist, I found myself working as a general reporter for the Paris Beacon-News and sitting in the corner to write for my own desk on my first day in 2014. Currently, I am the front desk supervisor at the Paris Rec Center, where I enjoy being part of a not-for-profit that services many people from the area and spreading my sarcasm around the office on all types of documents.

I have always loved books and writing. While my resume says that I've been working as a creative writer for several years, my habit of ordering numerous library books at a time is a continuous distraction. Semi-seriously, I've contemplated starting a Reading Anonymous group. When not trying to beat several deadlines, I enjoy recording my life's events as memoirs and other forms of creative writing. This is the first book to feature the byline of Kelly Nicholson.

DENISE SHUMAKER:

I grew up near Moonshine, Illinois on a sustainable farm in the house where my father was born. My father was devoted to my mom. He painted the house pink, my mom's favorite color. As a child, I rode in a pink Cadillac that my dad had painted for her. Because of my childhood years, I have always loved animals and had a deep interest in farm life.

My husband and I are retired and live on a small farm near Charleston, Illinois, where we have owned horses, llamas, goats, chickens, and cows. Over the years, I have also been known to take in many strays. We shared our love for animals with others through an educational therapeutic riding program for people who have disabilities.

I have had an interest in writing since grade school. When I was in third grade, one of my poems and illustrations was chosen and published in the statewide school news magazine. I was the artist for the school newspaper. I recently published a children's picture book that I wrote originally for my grandchildren. My grandchildren and I have enjoyed reading it together to their classmates.

LUZ WHITTENBARGER:

My father was a lawyer, and my mother was a published poet and activist for women's rights. We resided in Bogotá, Colombia.

I was educated in a Catholic school. I studied fine arts and architecture at the University of America in Bogotá. Traveling internationally was always my goal. I traveled to Central America and the United States in the early 1960s. I have also traveled to different parts of the world with my husband Bob, whom I met and married in Bogotá in 1964. We have two sons and four grandchildren, who are our life's greatest blessings.

I received my BA and teaching certification in Spanish from EIU in 1980 and taught at Lake Land College, then at Charleston High School and EIU. In 1980, I founded EIU's Summer of Excellence for Children with my dear friend Dorothy Swartzbaugh and directed it until 1986. I have served on the boards of several organizations, and I have done volunteer work, for which I received the Jefferson Award for Public Service in 2006. I love playing bridge, oil painting, gardening, decorating, and writing. This COVID-19 pandemic has stolen the pleasure of interacting with family and friends, but, in some ways, it has deepened my awareness of what I value most in life.

JACQUI WORDEN:

Mostly I write for myself. I write to record my life—my thoughts, my experiences, my observations, my inspirations, my hopes and dreams and prayers of daily gratitude. My morning pages, when I write them, are often directed to my Father-Mother God; the pages help me work through questions, conflicts, and personal plans.

Just as with my fifty-five-word story "The Shopping List," my life overflows with an abundance of things that bring me joy: family, friends, dogs, nature, books, tools and art supplies, games, rocking chairs, clay, collections of rocks and shells, paintings, music, images to capture with lens or pencil, travel, and opportunities to learn.

I am so grateful to have been a part of this Past~Forward writing community from its inception—a very sharing, caring group of individuals. It has been fun getting to know everyone and learning together.

YOANA YORDANOVA:

My name is Yoana Yordanova, and I wrote the piece "Once I Was Eight Years Old." I am sixteen years old, and I attend Charleston High School.

I recently started a writing club there for people like me who love to write. Writing can be quite therapeutic in the sense that it helps you escape the troubles of the world, but it also engages your imagination and creativity. Stories inspire people, and that's what makes writing special: the thought that your ideas can make someone smile or reflect. Generally, I like writing realistic fiction with a touch of sudden magic or dystopia. I really like the study of psychology and personality, so I try to explore that in the complexities of my characters. I've been writing for all my life, it seems, starting out with school assignments, and it slowly became a hobby. I also enjoy playing piano, singing in my high school choir, dancing in my ballet class, and being part of the debate club. I love doing these activities because they let me express and challenge myself. Something people might not know about me, though, is that I love listening to K-pop and classical music.

In Memoriam Biographies

BOB CLAPP:
(WRITTEN BY HIS DAUGHTER, TERESA BOES)

Bob Clapp was born February 6, 1936, in a house northwest of Oakland, Illinois. Shortly afterwards, the family moved to the edge of town down a dead-end street. The family didn't have it easy, but his dad kept food on the table by hunting and trapping. He had wonderful stories to tell of the shenanigans of growing up in a small town.

Bob married his high school sweetheart and had three children. He always kept his "young at heart" personality and enjoyed any activity with his children and grandchildren. He was known as Grandpa Bob to numerous children and adults alike. He touched the lives of many through his love of writing stories and poems and his tremendous faith in Jesus.

Bob had a love of life that didn't diminish even after being diagnosed with cancer. He is missed for his sense of humor and listening ear. We miss his wisdom, his tremendous faith, the sound of his infectious laughter, and his incredible ability to make friends anywhere he went. Bob lived by the quote by C.S. Lewis: "Has this world been so kind to you that you should leave with regret? There are better things ahead than any we leave behind."

MADELINE IGNAZITO:

(WRITTEN BY HER DAUGHTERS, KAREN CRIPPS AND SUSAN IGNAZITO-WILHEIM)

Madeline "Maddie" Ignazito was born and raised in Long Branch, New Jersey. She had an early affinity for math but was told that mathematics was a closed field for women. So she studied music, reasoning that music is an artistic application of math. Maddie earned a bachelor's and a master's in music composition and piano performance. She taught music from pre-K through college levels and was a piano teacher in her home studio for over forty years. Her composition "Variations and Fugue for Chamber Orchestra" received a national first-place prize. She and her husband, Martin "Marty" Ignazito, settled in Charleston in 1980 with their two daughters. She loved such intellectual pursuits as solving math puzzles and logic problems and reading Greek history and philosophy. She had creative hobbies as well, such as knitting, acting in CAT Theater productions, and writing. Her involvement with the Past~Forward Memoir Writing Group gave her an enormous sense of joy and accomplishment. Those who knew and loved her will remember her for her humor, caring heart, and passion for making the world a better place for all.

JOHNNI OLDS:
(WRITTEN BY HER HUSBAND, GLEN CRAWFORD)

Johnni was born in Kentucky, July 20, 1954. Her family moved to Mt. Carmel, Illinois, which she considered her hometown. During childhood, she endured two major back surgeries and the loss of her mother and a sister.

After high school, she moved to California. I met her there, and we married in 1975. We lived in San Francisco for thirty-five years, where Johnni found a spiritual home at Old First Presbyterian Church. She spent much of her time visiting and helping the elderly. Her health began to fail in the 1990s, and by 2009, we had to move. She wanted to be closer to family—her father and stepmother in Mt. Carmel and her sister Mary-Nance, who was indispensable in getting us settled in Charleston. Johnni found a new spiritual home at First Presbyterian Church of Charleston and continued her work with the elderly.

In October 2018, we took a road trip to Texas to visit friends and family. The trip put her in great spirits, but after we returned, her health took a turn for the worse. On New Year's Day 2019, she was taken from home to the ER for the last time. On January 30, 2019, she died.

May her faults be soon forgotten.

Her strength and courage,

Her kindness and generosity long remembered.

JULIA ANN HARTMAN REA:
(WRITTEN BY HER DAUGHTER AND SON)

Julia loved life. She would sometimes tease that she was a Valley girl, only to let you know in the next breath that she was referring to the Shenandoah Valley. Julia was enjoying her retirement from her career as a social worker and pursuing her passions.

She was a musician, artist, gardener, naturalist, writer, photographer, mother, grandmother, and great-grandmother. Her intense curiosity always kept her exploring and learning. You could write volumes with all the notes she scribbled on random slips of paper about some new bit of information she wanted to research later.

Julia loved people, and anyone she met didn't stay a stranger for very long. An extrovert-extraordinaire, she desired not only to meet new people but also to find ways to make them feel included—what a lovely character trait. Julia endured many hardships throughout her life but always persevered, searching to improve herself. She was so delighted to have found this memoir writing group, and she treasured the encouragement to write and the life-affirming friendships she gained as a result.

Made in the USA
Las Vegas, NV
16 December 2021

38230884R00144